THE UNICAMERAL LEGISLATURE

NEBRASKA OPENS ITS FIRST UNICAMERAL LEGISLATURE

THE UNICAMERAL LEGISLATURE

By

Alvin W. Johnson

LONDON · HUMPHREY MILFORD · OXFORD UNIVERSITY PRESS

THE UNIVERSITY OF MINNESOTA PRESS

Minneapolis

PREFACE

PUBLIC interest in the form and functioning of our state legislatures has grown consistently during the last twenty-five years. It was much intensified when Nebraska, in the fall of 1934, adopted a constitutional amendment abolishing her bicameral system and establishing a one-house legislature in its stead. No less than forty-two bills proposing some form of unicameral organization were introduced in twenty-one of the forty-three state legislatures which met in 1937. These developments, added to the perennial interest of students of government in legislative organization, seem to warrant a brief survey of the movement for unicameral legislatures.

I do not claim that this study is a definitive treatment of the subject, nor do I mean to imply that the single-chamber legislature is a cure for all our legislative ills. My purpose here is merely to assemble some of the historic arguments in support of the bicameral system, to present some of the criticisms that have been directed against it in practice, and to consider some of the proposed remedies, with special attention to the unicameral form.

I gratefully acknowledge the many helpful suggestions I have received from Walter McGovern, state senator of California; Ernest O. Voigt, member of the California assembly; H. V. Clayton, director of the California law and legislative reference section; George F. Williams, former lieutenant governor of Nebraska; Mulford Winsor, law and legislative reference librarian of Arizona; Mayo Fesler, director of the Citizens' League of Cleveland; and Norman H. Ford, secretary of the Ohio Single-House Legislature League. I also want to express my appreciation to L. Mark Hamilton and Helen B. Clapesattle for assisting me in the preparation of this work; to John W. Huling of the Commerce Clearing House for generously furnishing me with legislative bills and similar materials; to the Council of State Governments, the law and legislative reference librarians, the secretaries of state, and all others who have rendered specific service in the preparation of this material.

ALVIN W. JOHNSON

Angwin, California
December, 1937

CONTENTS

CONTENTS

ions. Size of legislature, electoral districts, term of
office, salaries, length and frequency of sessions, use
of nonpartisan ballot, use of initiative and referendum, impeachment procedure, relationship between executive and legislature, establishment of
legislative councils.

THE UNICAMERAL LEGISLATURE

LEGISLATURES ABROAD

MANKIND is prone to take established institutions for granted. As long as their mechanisms achieve our purposes without too much friction we accept their forms without question. But when they have become so corrupt or obsolete or ponderous that they block the advancement of personal interests and impede social progress, we are goaded into awareness of their structure; we look at them then with seeing eyes. Our American state legislatures seem to have reached this attention-compelling stage. Their two-house form stood almost without challenge for nearly a hundred years, but since the early years of the present century their inefficient methods and unsatisfactory laws have provoked an increasing consideration of their organization.

Why are our legislative bodies divided into two parts? Such a division is surely a clumsy and cumbersome addition to the governmental machinery. How did it come to be? What considerations impelled its adoption? Do these remain in force to justify its continuance? Is it necessary to good government? Questions like these are in the air today, and an attempt to answer them is in order.

Neither the bicameral system nor the attack upon it is peculiar to the United States. The English Parliament was the prototype for two-house legislatures; the story of its evolution through some six centuries provides a fund of arguments and examples for bicameralists; and its recent history is an important part of the widespread movement toward unicameralism. The eighteenth-century French philosophers made the first general attack upon the bicameral system;[1] the leaders of the French Revolution explicitly refused to adopt it; and the story of the French experiments with unicameral legislatures has given the opponents of the single chamber some of their most telling illustrations of its evils. For these reasons, at least a brief survey of the English and French experiences is necessary to an understanding of the American story and to an intelligent appraisal of the arguments for and against the two systems.

THE ENGLISH PARLIAMENT

The mistiness of long ago obscures the origin of the bicameral organization in the English Parliament. The traditional view, however, has based that origin upon the principle of estates, or social classes. It has long maintained that when Edward I summoned his Model Parliament in 1295, he intended it "to represent the three great estates or classes into which medieval society might be roughly divided, the clergy, the barons, and the commons; those who pray, those who fight, and those who work, as Maitland puts it."[2] The members might have been expected, therefore, to meet as three houses if not as one, but instead they resolved into two as the result of "a series of fortunate accidents."[3] The representatives of the lower clergy soon withdrew, preferring to vote their grants to the king in their own clerical assemblies, the convocations of Canterbury and York. The abbots and bishops, the Lords Spiritual, united with the earls and barons, the Lords Tem-

[1] The eighteenth-century Englishman Jeremy Bentham also attacked the two-house system in his great Constitutional Code. Incidentally, it was Bentham who first called that form the bicameral system.

[2] Sir Courtenay Ilbert, *Parliament, Its History, Constitution, and Practice* (London, 1911), p. 13.

[3] J. A. R. Marriott, *Second Chambers* (London, 1910), p. 6.

poral, to form the House of Lords. The knights of the shire, who might have been expected to join politically with the barons, on whose plane they belonged socially, chose instead to cast their lot with the representatives of the boroughs. The union of knights and burgesses came to constitute the House of Commons.

The democratic temper of modern American society would make the origin of the bicameral system in a cleavage between social classes an argument against it, but recent studies have raised doubts about this traditional interpretation. Albert F. Pollard expresses the newer view by calling the idea of three distinct and self-conscious estates in medieval England a myth imported later from the continent.[4] He maintains that Edward I knew nothing of either three estates or two houses, that there were six "grades" among the representatives, and that they all met together until the inconvenience of deliberating in so large a body moved the king to order separate assemblies, one of the lay lords with the clergy and the other of the knights with the burghers. Pollard insists that Parliament's taking on the form of two houses and three estates was due "not to any preconceived ideas about the value of a bicameral legislature or of a three-fold system of estates, but to the operation of royal writs and political convenience."[5] He points out that the coalition of the six grades into two houses would not have been likely if class lines had been deeply drawn.

Whatever the truth about its beginnings, by the time that Parliament had become the object of imitation by the

---

[4] *The Evolution of Parliament* (London, 1920), chaps. 3–6. For more evidence to support Pollard's position, see Albert B. White, "Some Early Instances of Concentration of Representatives in England," *American Historical Review,* 19:735–50 (July, 1914); William A. Morris, "The Beginnings of the House of Commons," *Pacific Historical Review,* 2:141–57 (June, 1933); and D. Pasquet, *An Essay on the Origins of the House of Commons* (Cambridge, England, 1935). There is an excellent brief summary of this position in Robert Luce, *Legislative Principles* (New York, 1930), p. 76.
[5] *The Evolution of Parliament,* p. 74.

American colonies and attack by the French philosophers,[6] its two houses were generally accepted as a reflection of the division of English society into a nobility and a commonalty. The House of Lords was an hereditary body whose members held their seats by right of birth into the English peerage,[7] and the House of Commons was an elected body, supposedly representative of the enfranchised commoners. To safeguard the privileges of its class was an acknowledged function of the upper house, which, until late in the seventeenth century, held legislative powers approximately coordinate with those of the lower house.

But the evolution of Parliament did not stop when that relationship between its houses had been attained. The main thread in parliamentary history during the last three centuries has been the gradual shearing of the Lords' power by the House of Commons, a development which reached a climax, though probably not a conclusion, in the Parliament Act of 1911. A review of this development will perhaps suggest that the process of amalgamation which made two houses out of the original six grades is continuing toward the absorption of the lords by the commons. It will surely demonstrate that "history seems to pronounce slowly but inexorably against the survival of the second chamber."[8]

The Puritan Revolution included an attempt to compress this development into one swift stroke, and the disastrous results are often cited by those who oppose unicameralism. When the rump parliament left by Pride's Purge had rid England of the monarchy, it proceeded against the aristocrats. By a vote of forty-four to twenty-

---

[6] See below, pages 11–12, 21, 26, 30.

[7] There were also representative and official elements in the House of Lords, the peers from Scotland and Ireland and the clergy, respectively; but the hereditary element far outnumbered them and it determined the character of the body in the public mind.

[8] J. H. Morgan, "Second Chambers," *Contemporary Review*, 97:533–44 (May, 1910).

nine the House of Commons declared on February 6, 1649, that "The House of Peers in Parliament is useless and dangerous and ought to be abolished. And that an Act be brought in to that purpose." [9] But this done, the Commons did not stop. They declared their power supreme in the land and sought to perpetuate themselves in office. They exercised both legislative and constituent powers with no regard for the civil liberties. They passed fanatical legislation. They lent themselves to an orgy of graft. Their tyrannical rule disgusted the people and angered Cromwell, who finally sent a squad of troopers to remove the speaker and the mace as an order of dismissal for what he called "the horridest arbitrariness that ever was in the world."

Those who use these events as a warning of the evils inherent in a single, unchecked chamber forget, perhaps, that the Rump was not the last of the legislative experiments during the Puritan Revolution. In his attempt to disguise the might of the sword with parliamentary forms, Cromwell called three more parliaments, the last of which was bicameral in form. But it was no more successful than the others. It may be that the difficulty lay, not with the form of legislature, but with the intolerance and hotheadedness of the men and the times.[10]

It is not necessary to detail the steps in the Commons' assumption of dominance over the restored House of Lords. The process was crowned during the eighteenth century by the development of the cabinet system, which put the powers shorn from the monarch in the hands of a ministry responsible solely to the lower house. When this had been achieved, only two circumstances made the structure of representative self-government still incomplete: the House of Commons was not a truly representative body and the

[9] G. M. Godden, "England's Single-Chamber Experiment," *Fortnightly Review,* 93:409–19 (March, 1910).

[10] G. B. Roberts, *The Functions of an English Second Chamber* (London, 1926), p. 24.

hereditary House of Lords held a veto over legislation. The first of these defects was corrected by the succession of reform bills in the nineteenth century. They extended the franchise and redistributed the parliamentary seats until the House of Commons finally became in fact what it appeared to be, a body of elected agents of the people, instead of henchmen of the lords who held boroughs in their pockets or otherwise controlled elections.

This adding the substance to the form of democracy is an important development in our story, because it forced a change in the acknowledged function of the upper house. Since a chamber existing to safeguard the privileges of a nobility would be an anomaly in a democratic society, the function of the House of Lords became that of protecting the people, of making sure that the elected chamber carried out the people's mandate. It no longer existed to oppose the people, but to be their ally, to hold in check the House of Commons when it was in danger of swerving from the path marked out by the general will.[11]

That was the theory which developed to justify the existence and the veto power of an unrepresentative and irresponsible house in the legislature of a representative democracy. In practice the powers of the House of Lords were exercised more and more along definite class and party lines. The upper chamber became the stronghold of the Tory and the Unionist parties and the implacable opponent of the Liberal party. It exercised its checking power with great vigor and vigilance when the Liberals were in power, but when its own party came into control it almost ceased to exist as far as any review or revision of bills was concerned. It was its stubborn and prolonged resistance to the program of social legislation sent up by the Liberal majority in the lower house that forced that majority to

[11] Hastings B. Lees-Smith, *Second Chambers in Theory and Practice* (London, 1923), p. 34.

contemplate drastic measures and occasioned a serious movement for the reform of the House of Lords.[12]

By 1906 the Labor party had included a plank in its platform calling for the abolition of the House of Lords and the institution of a unicameral legislature. In 1907 the House of Commons passed a resolution affirming the belief of the lower house that the upper house ought to be "so restricted by Law as to secure that within the limits of a single Parliament the final decision of the Commons shall prevail." [13] To which the Laborite Henderson moved the amendment that "the Upper House being an irresponsible part of the Legislature and of necessity representative only of interests opposed to the general well-being is a hindrance to national progress and ought to be abolished." [14]

Some of the lords, notably Lord Roseberry, saw how the wind was blowing and repeatedly introduced proposals for the reform of the House of Lords from within. All such proposals the lords received with cold indifference. They continued to block liberal legislation, daring finally to reject the Lloyd George budget of 1909. This was the last straw. Protest flamed throughout England, and the question became, "not is a reform of the second chamber necessary, but is a second chamber necessary?"[15] In 1911 the threat of packing the peerage was used to force the House of Lords into sanctioning the sharp curtailment of its powers incorporated in the Parliament Act of that year. According to its terms, a money bill which has passed the House of Commons becomes a law within one month, with or without the Lords' approval. Other bills which the Lords oppose become laws at the end of two years if passed by

[12] Roberts, *The Functions of an English Second Chamber*, pp. 167–210; Emily Allyn, *Lords versus Commons: A Century of Conflict, 1830–1930* (New York, 1931).

[13] Marriott, *Second Chambers*, p. 262.

[14] *Ibid.*, p. 261.

[15] Roberts, *The Functions of an English Second Chamber*, p. 9.

three successive sessions of the House of Commons. Since a suspensive veto is all that is left to the second chamber, there is reason for the claim that the English Parliament is now virtually a unicameral legislature.

But the reform of 1911 did not end the controversy. An attempt has been made to meet the arguments of the unicameralists by changing the constitution of the second chamber. In 1917 a Conference on the Reform of the Second Chamber was appointed. It was headed by Lord Bryce and included members from both houses. It did not result in any action since the members could not agree on a proposal, but its deliberations, reported to the prime minister in a letter from Lord Bryce, have provided fuel for the argument. The conference members agreed on four functions which remain to the second chamber, and the principal one of these is "the interposition of so much delay (and no more) in the passing of a bill into law as may be needed to enable the opinion of the nation to be adequately expressed upon it."[16] This has moved opponents to ask whether the function of merely interposing delay in the enacting of laws justifies such an expensive and complicated addition to the legislative machinery.[17]

The characteristics of the House of Lords which have drawn the fire of opponents in this argument are suggestive. They are: (1) *The wealth of the members.* To the claim of the defense that wealth provides the leisure necessary for a study of social problems and gives its possessors a stake in the country, the critics reply that wealth is more likely to result in idleness and self-indulgence and to give its holders a stake in "the heart" of the country. (2) *The class consciousness of the members.* They all belong to the same order and represent one interest. As Lord Roseberry told his fellows: "There is too much receiving of rent in

[16] Lees-Smith, *Second Chambers in Theory and Practice*, p. 33.
[17] *Ibid.*, pp. 44–45.

this House and too little paying of rent. We represent too much one class; we see one side of the shield too much." (3) *The hereditary nature of the body*. This is not only an embarrassing anomaly in a democratic government, but it interferes with the operation of representative, responsible, and party government. Liberal and socialist parties cannot secure a voice in the upper house without sacrificing their principles, and without such voice, control of the lower house does them little good. (4) *The great size of the body*. It numbers six hundred members, too many for efficient action or adequate deliberation. Observers state that unless there is a reform in these respects there is certain to be an act to abolish the House of Lords.[18]

LEGISLATURES IN FRANCE

To eighteenth-century Frenchmen, fretting under the yoke of an absolute monarchy, England was the ideal of self-government. They did not consider the defects of a limited franchise and a maldistribution of parliamentary seats; they saw only the machinery of election and representation, and it looked good to them. The admiration of such men as Montesquieu and Voltaire for the English system is well known. But there were other Frenchmen, especially those imbued with the fanatical democracy of Rousseau, who, while they admired self-government no less, withheld their approval from the English House of Lords. What right had it, or any second chamber, in representative government? Turgot was a leader in the attack on the bicameral system, pointing his strictures toward the adoption of the system by the American states and so bringing American statesmen to long, reasoned defenses.[19] The leaders of the French Revolution naturally inclined toward Turgot's views. Condorcet, Robespierre, and Sieyès were ardent unicameralists. They theorized that the bicameral

[18] Roberts, *The Functions of an English Second Chamber*, pp. 223–24.
[19] See below, page 30.

form violated the unity of sovereignty, that having two or more legislative chambers was equivalent to having two or more sovereign powers. In the words of Sieyès:

> The law is the will of the people; the people cannot at the same time have two different wills on the same subject; therefore, the legislative body which represents the people ought to be the essential one. Where there are two chambers, discord and division will be inevitable and the will of the people will be paralyzed by inaction.[20]

With his usual facility of phrase, Sieyès insisted that "it passes the wit of man to construct an effective Second Chamber" because "if a Second Chamber dissents from the first, it is mischievous; if it agrees with it, it is superfluous." Marriott has called this a superficial dilemma, but current opinion seems to consider it a practical one of considerable significance.[21]

The influence of these ideas on the revolutionists was helped along by the immediate circumstances. The medieval Estates-General had been tricameral in form, a house for each estate and one vote for each house. When the assembly was called again in 1789, after a recess of 175 years, the pivotal question was whether the old system of meeting and voting by order should be resumed or the assembly should meet in one house and vote by head. The former method would assure the control of the privileged classes, the latter that of the third estate. How the third estate won its point and the National Assembly became a unicameral body is a commonplace of history.

[20] Quoted in Edouard R. L. Laboulaye, *Questions constitutionelles*, p. 349. This idea resulted from a failure to recognize that the two chambers are complementary parts of a whole. Since the process of lawmaking is not complete until both houses have acted, the division into two chambers does not split the sovereignty any more than does the division into executive and legislative departments. It is now generally admitted that as long as legislation emanates from the assembly as a whole, there is unity of sovereignty.

[21] Marriott, *Second Chambers*, p. 1. See below, pages 61–63.

All of the Revolution's assemblies up to 1795, whether constituent or legislative, were unicameral. The turmoil and violence which they countenanced and sometimes authorized are stock illustrations for anti-unicameralists. They maintain that a second chamber would have prevented the worst excesses of the Revolution and they point with vigor to the restoration of a bicameral legislature under the Directory as a sign of returning political health. The question can be only academic, for it is beyond possibility to imagine the fanatical democrats of the Revolution tolerating a second chamber made up of aristocrats, and a second chamber of men like themselves would not have been much help.

The Second Republic and the Third Republic both established single chambers. In 1848 the experiment was unsatisfactory; the legislature was charged with "violence, instability, and excesses of the worst kind" and with permitting Napoleon III to make himself dictator. The last point carries little weight now that two-house legislatures have offered no serious obstacle to either Mussolini or Hitler. The unicameral National Assembly which sat during the early years of the Third Republic made a more creditable record. During its five years of service it succeeded in concluding peace with Germany; in putting down the Paris Commune; in paying the indemnity, which freed France from German occupation; and, through the constituent authority it assumed, in giving the republic its constitutional laws. These laws re-established the bicameral system. Why? The question is all the more pertinent because the republican tradition in France had consistently favored the unicameral form.

The National Assembly was overwhelmingly monarchist in sentiment. It wished to make France a constitutional monarchy, but when the hopes of an immediate restoration were wrecked by the Count de Chambord's clinging so tenaciously to the Bourbon lily that he prevented a compromise between Legitimists and Orleanists, the National Assembly set itself reluctantly to the task of giving the republic a constitutional foundation. Considering the restoration of the monarchy only deferred, however, the assembly planned a monarchist senate to counteract the influence of a republican chamber of deputies. One-fourth of the senators were to be chosen for life, originally by the National Assembly and subsequently by the senate itself, and the rest were to be elected indirectly by an electoral college weighted in favor of the rural communes, since these were the strongholds of monarchist sympathies and the cities were the centers of radical republicanism. How well the assembly planned was shown in the strongly monarchist complexion of the first senate, which supported President Macmahon when he dismissed the obstreperous republican chamber. But the electors were for the republic. They gave its supporters a decisive victory at the polls; Macmahon resigned; and a few years later the senate was reformed. Its life memberships were abolished and a graded system of representation was established which would favor neither the rural communes nor the large cities.[22] Since that time the French senate has been a bulwark of strength for the republic, but it too has served as a conservative stronghold tending to delay progressive social legislation.

THE EXTENT OF UNICAMERALISM

France was not the only nation to admire the Englishman's freedom from arbitrary rule. That freedom was the envy of the world and envying, the world took to copying. It copied not only the freedom but the system that seemed to achieve it, and the bicameral legislature spread alongside representative government during the nineteenth century. A few states, Spain, Portugal, Mexico, Bolivia, Ecua-

[22] Lees-Smith, *Second Chambers in Theory and Practice*, pp. 141–48.

dor, and Peru, adopted single chambers at first; but they soon abandoned them and joined the bicameralist ranks. When the second decade of the twentieth century opened, the only states having unicameral legislatures were Greece, Luxemburg, Serbia, a few of the smaller German states, some of the Swiss cantons, and the Canadian provinces of Ontario, Manitoba, and British Columbia.[23]

Since the World War, however, there has been a marked increase in the number of single-house legislatures. Even where new constitutions have provided for bicameral bodies, they have tended to decrease the powers of the upper chamber. Jugoslavia, Bulgaria, Turkey, Finland, Esthonia, Latvia, and Lithuania, all established single houses, and the Spanish constitution of 1931 added the Cortes to their number. On the other hand, Poland set up two chambers, although the act carried by a very narrow margin. The Irish Free State also chose the bicameral system in spite of the difficulties it had encountered in the English House of Lords. It abolished its upper house in 1936 but restored it in the constitution adopted in July, 1937. Fascist Italy and Nazi Germany both have two-house legislatures, but a legislature of any kind in those states is only a matter of form. The new Soviet constitution retained the bicameral system for the U.S.S.R., making all decisions of the executive Council of People's Commissars subject to the approval of the legislative Supreme Council.[24] However, there is no provision in the constitution to prevent the Politbureau of the Communist party from determining legislative policies in the future as it has in the past. Norway's legislature belongs to neither the bicameral nor the unicameral system, but to both.

Outside Europe, eight of the Canadian provinces and

---

[23] J. N. Larned, compiler, *New Larned History for Ready Reference, Reading, and Research* (12 vols., Springfield, Massachusetts, 1922–24), 2:1014.

[24] Constitution of 1936, chap. 3.

Queensland, Australia, are unicameralist, as are also several of the provinces of Argentina and the Latin American republics of Costa Rica, Guatemala, Honduras, Panama, and El Salvador. To this group we may now add the Philippine Islands and the American state of Nebraska. Before turning to the United States, however, we may profitably consider in more detail the anomalous Norwegian Storthing, the Canadian provincial legislatures, and the Philippine constitution.

The Norwegian Storthing. — The special interest in Norway's legislature, the Storthing, is due to the fact that the members of the second chamber are elected by the legislature itself. This practice is being commended by students of legislative organization as a way of securing the benefits of the two-house system without its disadvantages. The Storthing is elected as a single assembly, but its first task is to choose one-fourth of its members to form the Lagthing, or upper house. The rest of the members constitute the Odelsthing, or lower house. The purpose of this practice is not to create a second chamber but to ensure added care in the consideration of specified types of legislation. For financial measures and constitutional alterations, the Storthing acts as one body without separation into its two parts. The Lagthing has no power to initiate legislation; it can only consider those bills which the Odelsthing refers to it. If it rejects them, they are returned to the Odelsthing for a second consideration and, if necessary, to the Storthing as a whole for the final decision.[25] In spite of its limited power and committee-like appearance, the Lagthing should not be considered a legislative council.[26] It exercises true legislative functions.

Unicameralism in the Canadian provinces. — Since Canada has attained federation and autonomy, her several prov-

[25] Lees-Smith, *Second Chambers in Theory and Practice,* chap. 9.
[26] For a definition and description of the legislative council, see page 82.

inces have shown no blind aping of the mother country in their legislative structures. Ontario, British Columbia, Alberta, and Saskatchewan have operated under single chambers since the beginning of their existence as separate states. The others have tried upper houses both of members nominated by the governor general and of elected representatives. Coming to feel that the first was out of place in representative government and that the second was an unnecessary duplication, all but Quebec turned to unicameral legislatures. Manitoba began with a nominated upper chamber but abolished it six years later. New Brunswick followed suit in 1892. Prince Edward Island tried the nominated chamber first, made it elective in 1862, and finally merged it with the lower house in 1893. It has retained some differentiation of members in its single chamber, however, for part of them are elected on a property franchise and part on adulthood suffrage.[27]

Nova Scotia struggled for many years to get rid of its upper house. In 1890, after that body had refused to vote itself away, the lieutenant governor packed it with members pledged to vote for its extinction. Once in office, however, the new members developed scruples about the procedure and the project fell through. It was revived in 1926. This time the new members fulfilled the purpose of their nomination, and the bill for its own abolition was passed by the upper house on February 29, 1928. That has left only Quebec bicameral, and recent events indicate that the second house is not assured of its existence even there.

Since the analogy between the provinces of federal Canada and the states of the federal United States is often pointed out by those who would make our state legislatures

---

[27] W. P. M. Kennedy, *The Constitution of Canada* (London, 1922), pp. 390–91. See also Arch B. Clark, "The Single-Chamber Legislature of Manitoba," *National Municipal Review*, 13:225–33 (April, 1924), and George M. Wrong, "The Single-House Legislature of Ontario," *National Municipal Review*, 13:169–72 (March, 1924).

unicameral, two points at which the analogy fails should be noted. First, in the United States the upper houses are all elected and there is no responsible government, as there is in all the Canadian provinces. Consequently the argument that a second chamber interferes with the functioning of democratic government cannot be argued on the same basis here as in Canada. Second, the Canadian assemblies exercise constituent as well as legislative powers; that is, the constitution of any Canadian province can be altered by a simple act of the provincial legislature. This gives the Canadian chamber power which would not adhere to single chambers in the United States. Yet there has been no instance of legislative despotism in Canada, and there is no public demand for the restoration of the second-chamber check. The safeguard of an immediate and direct appeal to the electors by dissolving the chamber and calling new elections has been sufficient.

The Philippine constitution. — The new constitution creating the Philippine Commonwealth is especially interesting, not only because it was adopted with the sanction of the United States but also because it includes a number of features that we shall find recurring in unicameralist proposals in our own states. It vests the legislative power in a one-house National Assembly of 120 members elected for three years. The legislative sessions are to be held annually but are limited to one hundred days. The assembly elects its own speaker and secretary. Its acts are subject to presidential veto, but it may override that by a two-thirds vote, except in a few specified cases. Impeachment, the confirmation of presidential appointments, and other duties which usually devolve upon second chambers are to be performed by special commissions elected by and from the assembly.[28]

[28] See Jesus Occeña, "A Unicameral Legislature for the Philippines," *Philippine Law Journal*, 13:157–76 (November, 1933), and David H. Popper, "Creating a Philippine Commonwealth," *Foreign Policy Reports*, 12:234–44 (December 15, 1936).

2

EARLY LEGISLATURES IN THE
UNITED STATES

NEBRASKA's departure from the bicameral norm has been
commonly hailed as an experiment. This is a natural and,
in spite of Senator Norris' objection, probably accurate
designation, but it is likely to be misleading. As we have
seen, the unicameral legislature is not new in the world.
And it is not new in America. During the seventeenth century the American colonial legislatures were, almost without exception, unicameral in form. But one by one they
became bicameral, until by 1763 only Pennsylvania and
Delaware had single chambers. When the colonies became
independent states, they kept the two-house form, and
when they organized a federal union, they made their national legislature bicameral too. Pennsylvania, Georgia,
and Vermont were the only states to adopt the single house,
and all three of them had added second chambers by 1836.
From that time until 1934, bicameralism was the rule without an exception in the United States. Each phase of this
development has fact or theory to contribute to the current
discussion of legislative organization.

THE COLONIAL LEGISLATURES

In most of the colonies, when the insistent demand of
the colonists secured for them the right to participate in
formulating government policies, their representatives

joined with the colonial governor and his council of assistants in a single legislative body.[1] But the two groups do not seem to have fused. The feeling developed, both in the public mind and among the legislators, that the magistrates were the spokesmen of the rulers, royal or proprietary, and that only the deputies were the agents of the people. This differentiation was logical where the officials were appointed, but it was present even where they were elected. It was undoubtedly intensified in such colonies as Massachusetts, Rhode Island, and Connecticut, where the officials and the deputies were elected by different constituencies, the former at large and the latter from specific districts.

The idea that the members of the single assembly represented two different orders expressed itself in certain practices which led naturally to the separation into two houses. For instance, in 1636 the Massachusetts General Court made itself virtually two bodies by requiring the approval of a majority of each group, the magistrates and the deputies, to make an act valid. The short step from this requirement to the bicameral form was taken eight years later in an act that divided the General Court into two houses, meeting and voting separately.

In North Carolina the constitution of 1670 provided for a unicameral body comprising five deputies appointed by the proprietor and twenty representatives chosen by the people, but it required that all laws must be approved by the governor and at least three of the deputies. This assigning of special authority to the proprietor's deputies must have suggested their ultimate withdrawal into a separate

[1] New York and possibly South Carolina were the exceptions. Coming to the English from the Dutch, New York did not get representative government until 1683, when the change to the bicameral system was already well under way in the other colonies. Whether South Carolina's legislature was ever unicameral is uncertain. For a detailed account of the colonial legislatures, see Thomas F. Moran, *The Rise and Development of the Bicameral System in America* (Baltimore, 1895).

chamber. In Rhode Island the process of division began when the deputies were given permission to meet for half an hour prior to the opening of the general assembly in order that they might consider such matters as were for the "well beinge of the Collony." In Connecticut the preliminary step was an action authorizing the governor, deputy governor, and magistrates to act as a standing council during the intervals when the general assembly was not in session. Later the practice developed of submitting only the important measures to the assembly, and the bicameral form was soon established.

The influence of the English Parliament in this development is not to be minimized. The example of the House of Commons was often cited by the deputies in their requests for separate organization. But the example of Parliament served as a suggestion of separation when dissension arose between the deputies and the magistrates rather than as a cause of the original differentiation between them. The circumstances in New Jersey illustrate this. The frame of government drawn up by the proprietors in 1665 vested the legislative power in an assembly comprising the governor, from six to twelve councilors, and twelve deputies elected by the people. At the first meeting of the assembly in 1668 there were ten deputies present, but only seven councilors. Knowing that they would be outvoted in a single assembly, the councilors insisted upon meeting apart. But the reason they gave was a desire to imitate the English Parliament.[2]

These were the customs and influences that gave rise to the bicameral form in America. By 1763 all of the colonies except Pennsylvania and Delaware had two chambers. In the royal colonies it had become the custom for the king to appoint the governor and his assistants, who formed the

[2] Moran, *The Rise and Development of the Bicameral System in America,* p. 28.

upper house and represented the royal prerogative. The members of the lower house were elected by the colonists who had the franchise. In the proprietary colonies, the proprietor appointed the governor and his council, subject to the king's approval. The council exercised both executive and judicial powers and shared the legislative power with the assembly. Its members were usually appointed from the wealthy and landowning classes upon the recommendation of the governor. The right to initiate all legislation usually rested with the upper house, but the colonists were objecting to this custom, especially to the right of the council to initiate revenue measures. They insisted that bills dealing with the raising and spending of money should originate with the people's representatives. Conflicts of this sort tended to define the division between the two houses.

THE EARLY STATE LEGISLATURES

This being the situation when the Declaration of Independence necessitated the establishment of state governments, those governments naturally included two-house legislatures. Between 1776 and 1781, eleven of the thirteen states framed new constitutions,[3] and nine of the eleven made their legislatures bicameral. Pennsylvania retained the one-house assembly in her constitution of 1776, and Georgia adopted the single chamber in her constitution of 1777. Vermont also set up a unicameral legislature in the constitution she adopted in 1777, although she was not admitted as a state until 1791.[4]

We ought not to let the avowed scorn of the early Americans for the trappings of royalty and aristocracy lead us into the misapprehension that theirs was a democratic society. That their social distinctions were based on wealth instead of on birth and were not legally recognized, except

[3] Connecticut and Rhode Island continued to use their colonial charters and did not draw up new constitutions until the nineteenth century.

[4] For further description of these legislatures, see pages 32–44.

for the line between freemen and slaves and indentured servants, makes less real difference than has sometimes been supposed. The significance of this in our present discussion is that these social distinctions played a part in the adoption of the bicameral form for the early legislatures. The upper house was a convenient device for the special representation of wealth and property. A few facts about suffrage qualifications will make this clear.

There were two general types of political restrictions in the early American communities, one on the right to vote and another on the right to hold office. Both of these types were achieved largely by property qualifications, and within each of them different requirements might be imposed to mark off the senators from the representatives. To illustrate: In North Carolina any freeman who paid taxes could vote for members of the lower house, but only those who possessed freeholds of at least fifty acres could vote for senators. To be eligible for election to the lower house a man must own not less than one hundred acres, but he must own at least three hundred to be eligible for the senate.

Not all of these gradations were present in every state. Some omitted the difference in suffrage requirements and others in the qualifications for office, but all of them established one or the other. Massachusetts, for example, permitted anyone with an estate worth sixty pounds or producing an income of three pounds to vote for the members of both houses; but it restricted senate membership to those with property worth six hundred pounds, while an estate worth two hundred pounds made one eligible to a seat in the house of representatives.[5] It is interesting to note that Thomas Jefferson objected to Virginia's maintaining the

[5] For a comprehensive study of these qualifications, see Albert E. McKinley, *The Suffrage Franchise in the Thirteen English Colonies in America* (Philadelphia, 1905). There is a brief but adequate summary in Charles A. Beard, *The Economic Interpretation of the Constitution of the United States* (New York, 1929), chap. 4. See also Franklin L. Riley, *Colonial Origins of New England Senates* (Baltimore, 1896).

same qualifications for the electors of both houses. He said that two houses representing the same electorate served no useful purpose and that if the lower house could not be chosen by a broader electorate, one of the houses was superfluous and should be dispensed with — which was recognizing in practice one horn of Sieyès' theoretical dilemma.[6]

Although such restrictions disfranchised fewer people proportionately at that time than they would today, their effects were noticeable even then. New York's restrictions, for instance, kept about one-third of the potential voters away from the polls. In that state the senators were elected by those having a freehold worth one hundred pounds or more and the representatives by those having a freehold of twenty pounds or renting a tenement worth at least forty shillings. According to the census of 1790, only 1,209 of New York's 30,000 residents owned freeholds of one hundred pounds or more; only 1,221 had freeholds of twenty pounds or more; and only 2,661 were forty-shilling freeholders. The state's potential vote was shown in the election of 1788. Members of the convention which was to ratify the federal constitution and members of the state assembly were chosen at the same election, but the former were chosen by universal manhood suffrage and the latter under the usual restriction. As a result, one successful candidate received 2,677 votes as a member of the convention and only 1,500 votes as a member of the assembly. In Albany County the vote for assembly members ran consistently about 1,600 under that for convention members.[7]

The amount of the property qualifications varied widely from state to state. South Carolina's requirements were the highest. In that state the suffrage was restricted to those who owned at least fifty acres; senators had to own an

[6] Arthur N. Holcombe, *State Government in the United States* (New York, 1931), p. 68.
[7] Beard, *An Economic Interpretation of the Constitution*, pp. 67–68.

estate worth at least two thousand pounds; and representatives must own property worth at least one thousand pounds. Pennsylvania and Georgia, the states with single chambers, had the most extended suffrage. Yet even in Pennsylvania only those who paid taxes could vote. Georgia required property worth at least two hundred and fifty pounds for the members of its assembly, but gave the franchise to every white male owning property worth ten pounds or "being of any mechanic trade." Virginia too omitted the property requirement in the case of "certain artisans residing in Norfolk and Williamsburg."

These facts make it clear that the barriers to universal manhood suffrage in the early American states served as a defense for property rights and that in most states the senate gave special representation to wealth. The representation of mere man was left to the lower house. We shall see that this was a conscious purpose in the formation of the second chamber and not merely a chance development.

THE FEDERAL CONGRESS

Thus was the legislative stage set when the federal convention met in Philadelphia in 1787 and drew up a constitution which fashioned the federal legislature on the bicameral pattern. The two-house form of the national congress has not been attacked in the current controversy, but inquiring how it came to be is pertinent to our discussion nonetheless. It was an important factor in the adoption of that form for the legislatures of new states coming into the union, and its story shows the reasons which were thought to justify the bicameral system at that time. Our knowledge of why the framers of the Constitution made the legislature bicameral is drawn from the fragmentary records we have of the convention debates and from the argumentative literature produced during the conflict over ratification. In the latter category the *Federalist,* written by

Hamilton and Madison for the electorate of New York but widely circulated in other states as well, is a comprehensive and logical defense of the Constitution and its provisions, including the bicameral legislature.

Occasional references to the English Parliament by convention members show that the example of that institution was not without effect, but more important because less remote was the example of the bicameral system in most of the states from which the members came. It was the system with which they were familiar, and they tended naturally to reproduce it. Into the balance on the same side went the weight of their experience with the Congress under the Articles of Confederation. That was a unicameral body, and although its one-house form can hardly be blamed for its specific weaknesses, the unicameral system suffered in the minds of the convention members from its association with the evils that had brought the states to the point of framing a new government. But these examples must be counted as influences rather than as causes; that is, they suggested the way, or the way not, to achieve the desired ends. The causes are to be found in the practical advantages that the bicameral system seemed to offer.

There was the advantage of the two kinds of representation that a two-house structure permits in a federal form of government. This advantage was used to break the deadlock between the small and the large states and thus removed one of the chief obstacles to agreement in the convention. The Virginia Plan proposed that membership in both houses of the legislature be proportionate to population, which would have given control to the larger states. The small states countered with the New Jersey Plan of a single chamber in which all the states would have equal voting strength. The Connecticut Compromise used the bicameral form to satisfy the small states with equal representation in the Senate and the large states with proportionate representation in the House of Representatives. This advantage would not seem to pertain to bicameral state legislatures, but the idea has appeared in the representation afforded in state senates to county units or other distinct sections.[8]

The two-house form also made possible an external check on the power of the executive and an internal check on that of the legislature. The delegates to the convention wanted a strong federal government because of the benefits it could provide, such as a sound currency and protection for shipping; but they were suspicious and distrustful of all government agencies. Their experiences with the colonial governors made them want to restrict the power of the executive. So they gave him the Senate as a sort of advisory council, which would confirm his appointments to office and guard against his mistakes in making treaties. But they were also afraid of an unchecked legislature, as the following excerpt from the *Federalist* will show:

The legislative department is everywhere extending the sphere of its activity, and drawing all power into its impetuous vortex. The founders of our republic . . . seem never for a moment to have turned their eyes from the danger to liberty from the overgrown and all-grasping prerogative of an hereditary branch of the legislative authority. They seem never to have recollected the danger from legislative usurpations, which, by assembling all power in the same hands, might lead to the same tyranny as is threatened by executive usurpations.[9]

The organization in two houses, each having the power to check the legislation of the other, was deemed an excellent arrangement for preventing any such legislative usurpations — though the device of judicial review was added, to make assurance doubly sure.

Not only did the constitution-makers fear the tyranny of government; they feared that of the people even more.

[8] See below, pages 53, 65.
[9] *The Federalist*, No. 48.

They were, almost without exception, members of the upper, propertied classes. They were alarmed by such signs of incipient democracy as Shay's Rebellion, which had recently occurred in Massachusetts. To them, democracy was synonymous with "confusion and licentiousness." This is not our interpretation; it is explicit in their own statements, as a few examples will demonstrate. According to Madison's notes, John Dickinson, for instance, argued for a restriction of suffrage to freeholders. "He considered them the best guardians of liberty; And the restriction of the right to them as a necessary defense agst. the dangerous influence of those multitudes without property & without principle, with which our Country like all others, will in time abound." [10]

Gouverneur Morris objected to the Constitution at one stage because "it threatens this Country with an Aristocracy. The Aristocracy will grow out of the House of Representatives. Give the vote to the people who have no property, and they will sell them to the rich who will be able to buy them. . . . The time is not distant when this Country will abound with mechanics & manufacturers who will receive their bread from their employers. Will such men be the secure & faithful Guardians of liberty? Will they be the impregnable barrier agst. aristocracy?" [11]

But here as elsewhere the best statement of the common opinion was made by Alexander Hamilton:

All communities divide themselves into the few and the many. The first are the rich and well born, the other the mass of the people. The voice of the people has been said to be the voice of God; and however generally this maxim has been quoted and believed, it is not true in fact. The people are turbulent and changing; they seldom judge or determine right. Give therefore to the first class a distinct, permanent share in the government. They will check the unsteadiness of the second, and as they

[10] Quoted in Beard, *An Economic Interpretation of the Constitution*, p. 195.

[11] *Ibid.*, pp. 207–08.

cannot receive any advantage by a change, they therefore will ever maintain good government. Can a democratic assembly who annually resolve in the masses of people, be supposed steadily to pursue the public good? Nothing but a permanent body can check the imprudence of democracy.[12]

These quotations express not only a fear of the people but the idea that the establishment of a second chamber which would not be subject to direct popular control would be a way of restraining the people's pernicious influence. This conception of the Senate as a bulwark of the "natural aristocracy," the propertied classes, against "turbulent democracy," the property-less masses, recurs again and again in the speeches and writings of the Federalists. George Mason told the convention that "one important object in constituting the senate was to secure the rights of property." [13] General Charles Cotesworth Pinckney proposed that no salary be paid to senators, because since that branch, he said, "was meant to represent the wealth of the country, it ought to be composed of persons of wealth; and if no allowance was to be made, the wealthy alone would undertake the service." [14] Edmund Randolph's remarks on the structure of the Senate, as reported by Madison, carry the same idea:

If he was to give an opinion as to the number of the second branch, he should say that it ought to be much smaller than that of the first, so small as to be exempt from the passionate proceedings to which numerous assemblies are liable. He observed that the general object was to provide a cure for the evils under which the U. S. laboured; that in tracing these evils to their origin every man had found it in the turbulence and follies of democracy: that some check was to be sought for agst. this tendency of our governments: and that a good Senate seemed most likely to answer the purpose. . . . The Democratic licentiousness of the State legislatures proved the neces-

[12] *Ibid.*, p. 199.
[13] *Ibid.*, p. 206.
[14] *Ibid.*, pp. 211–12.

sity of a firm Senate. The object of this 2d. branch is to controul the democratic branch of the Natl. Legislature. If it be not a firm body, the other branch being more numerous and coming directly from the people, will overwhelm it.[15]

All of which Hamilton summed up succinctly when he wrote: "The necessity of a senate is not less indicated by the propensity of all single and numerous assemblies, to yield to the impulse of sudden and violent passions, and to be seduced by factious leaders into intemperate and pernicious resolutions."[16]

The bicameral form was not without opponents, however. The attacks of Turgot and his fellows were having an effect upon some American thinkers, notably Benjamin Franklin, who likened the bicameral system to a cart with a horse hitched to each end pulling in opposite directions.[17] It may have been Franklin's influence that was responsible for Pennsylvania's negative vote, or it may have been the effect of a unicameralist example at home.[18]

The second alternative is suggested by the fact that one of the best pieces of argumentation against the ratification of the Constitution was the famous Centinel letters in Pennsylvania. Their author would have none of the Federalist theory of "balanced economic interests and innocu-

[15] *Ibid.*

[16] *The Federalist,* No. 62.

[17] See above, page 11. It was in answer to Turgot's attack and to counteract its influence and Franklin's that John Adams wrote a lengthy defense of the American state constitutions, showing that the single chambers of history had been visionary and corrupt and had "usually ended in despotism." See "A Defense of the Constitutions of Government of the United States of America, against the Attack of M. Turgot, in His Letter to Dr. Price, 22 March, 1778." This constitutes volumes IV–VI of *The Works of John Adams* (Charles F. Adams, editor, 10 vols., Boston, 1850–56).

[18] Some writers, Madison among them, have contended that the Pennsylvania delegates actually favored two chambers, since Pennsylvania changed to the bicameral system in 1790, but that they voted against the system in the convention in deference to Franklin. See Jonathan Elliot, *Debates in the Several State Conventions on the Adoption of the Federal Constitution* (5 vols., Philadelphia, 1836–59), 5:165.

ous legislatures." He disapproved of deliberately setting property interests against each other in the legislature and thought that faith in "the political capacity of the broad undifferentiated mass of the community should be the basis of the constitution." He stated so well a favorite argument of contemporary unicameralists that the passage is worth quoting:

The highest responsibility is to be attained in a simple structure of government, for the great body of the people never steadily attend to the operations of government, and for the want of due information are liable to be imposed upon. If you complicate the plan by various orders, the people will be perplexed and divided in their sentiment about the sources of abuses or misconduct; some will impute it to the senate, others to the house of representatives, and so on, that the interposition of the people may be rendered imperfect or perhaps wholly abortive. But if imitating the constitution of Pennsylvania, you vest all the legislative power in one body of men (separating the executive and the judicial), elected for a short period, and necessarily excluded by rotation from permanency and guarded from precipitancy and surprise by delays imposed on its proceedings, you will create the most perfect responsibility; for then, whenever the people feel a grievance, they cannot mistake the authors and will apply the remedy with certainty and effect, discarding them at the next election.[19]

But the majority of those who had a voice in the adoption of the Constitution agreed with the bicameralists rather than with the Centinel writer, and the federal congress was given a two-chamber form. This influenced the three states that still had single chambers. Pennsylvania and Georgia added upper houses in 1790, Vermont followed in 1836, all of the new states carved from the public domain adopted the legislative system of their older sisters, and the bicameral system became a political axiom in America. Now that it is being challenged once again we may ask how the single

[19] Quoted in Beard, *An Economic Interpretation of the Constitution,* p. 315.

chamber worked in the three states that kept it long enough for a fair trial.[20]

Georgia. — The first legislative authority in the colony of Georgia, established by the charter of 1732, was a single chamber.[21] But when the proprietors surrendered their rights in 1752 and the colony became a royal province, the legislature was made bicameral. That form endured until independence was achieved. Upon the recommendation of the Continental Congress that each state draw up a new frame of government, a state convention was called to draft a constitution. This constitution restored the unicameral system in Georgia. It established a chamber of members elected from the counties on the basis of population for a term of one year. Some of the larger towns were given special representation, and the delegates elected to the national congress were given seats and permitted to debate and vote in the state assembly.

Following the custom of the early state governments, the constitution conferred extensive powers on the legislature and carefully circumscribed the power of the executive. It authorized the assembly to determine its own rules of procedure, to elect the governor and the executive council, and to legislate for the general welfare of the state. But proposed bills were to be submitted to the governor and council for their comments or amendments.

Soon after Georgia had ratified the federal Constitution, the state legislature authorized the election of delegates to a constitutional convention, since it was found necessary

[20] Some authorities object to calling these legislatures unicameral since each of them had a council of censors which possessed many of the powers and duties of a second chamber.

[21] William B. Stevens, *A History of Georgia* (2 vols., Philadelphia, 1859); Charles C. Jones, *The History of Georgia* (2 vols., Boston, 1883) ; Hugh M'Call, *The History of Georgia* (Atlanta, 1909).

to bring the state government into "harmonious action" with the new federal government and "to remedy certain defects in the practical workings" of the constitution under which Georgia had been operating since 1777.[22] After passing the scrutiny of three different conventions, a new state constitution was adopted on May 4, 1790. It made the legislature bicameral.

As we have indicated, Georgia's purpose in revising her government was to make it more comformable to the federal Constitution. There can be little question that the choice of the two-house form for the national legislature was a powerful factor in influencing Georgia to adopt the bicameral system. How much part actual dissatisfaction with the one-house form played in the change is hard to determine. The strife and turmoil under which a province so newly independent tried to establish a government and participate in a war simultaneously make it difficult to evaluate what was at best a modified form of unicameralism. Perhaps the most significant fact is that although a number of attempts were made to bring the executive council, and in some instances the governor, into ill repute, comparatively little criticism was directed against the single-chamber assembly. There is reason for the claim that, had there not been the precedent of the bicameral legislature in the federal government, the unicameral form might have been retained when Georgia's constitution was revised.

Pennsylvania. — From 1682 to 1701 the colonial legislature of Pennsylvania was bicameral. But the Charter of Privileges, which William Penn, the proprietor, granted in 1701, when he was leaving the colony for the last time, gave to Pennsylvania — and to Delaware[23] — a legislature of one chamber, called the Assembly. The charter could be

[22] Stevens, *History of Georgia*, 2:388.
[23] In 1682 the Duke of York gave to Penn the proprietorship of Delaware.

amended by a vote of six-sevenths of the assembly, without the consent of the governor, except for the clauses guaranteeing religious liberty, which were not subject to change. The assembly's membership consisted of four representatives from each county elected annually by the freemen of the province. It determined its own time for meeting and could not be prorogued by the governor. Provision was made for a council appointed by the proprietor, which was to serve as an advisory body to the governor and which might also in certain cases act as a court of appeals. In the event of a vacancy in the governorship, the president of the council was to act as governor.

The people made no effort to change the charter until they gained their independence in the Revolution. But by the middle of the eighteenth century there was considerable dissatisfaction with the distribution of representation in the assembly. By 1764 there were eight counties in the colony, but the three original counties of Philadelphia, Chester, and Bucks had twenty-six of the thirty-six members in the legislature. In 1776 these three counties, with one-third of the population, had twenty-four members, while the rest of the counties, with two-thirds of the population, had only fourteen members. This situation was the result of not reapportioning membership in the assembly as the colony expanded westward, and it aroused much opposition in the frontier counties. Unequal representation was also causing discontent in the city of Philadelphia, which was still represented in the assembly by the original allotment of two members. Further unrest was due to the fact that the passage of a very narrow suffrage qualification enabled the Quakers to retain control, although they were

which was united with Pennsylvania for many years. When it was granted a legislature of its own in 1703, it followed Pennsylvania's example by adopting a unicameral assembly, which it kept until 1776. Its state constitution, made in that year, established the bicameral system.

being outnumbered by the influx of immigrants from all over Europe.

In the midst of this discontent came independence and the need for establishing a new state government. The constitutional convention sat in Philadelphia from June to September, 1776. It vested the legislative power of the new state in a single chamber, in which representation was based on the number of taxable inhabitants and which was to be chosen by an electorate extended to include all freemen who had reached the age of twenty-one, had resided in the state for one year, and had been listed on the tax rolls. The convention provided for a multiple executive, a council of twelve members elected for three years. In a joint session with the legislature, the council was to choose one of its own members to serve as chairman of the council and to be known as the President of Pennsylvania, but not to have any more power than the other councilors. The convention also set up a council of censors, a sort of inquisitorial body which was to keep watch on the enforcement of the laws and which was given the power to call a convention when constitutional revision seemed necessary.

It is an indication of unusual satisfaction with the single chamber that this convention of 1776 retained it, because the convention was dominated by a group of radical Whigs, whose revolutionary tendencies are evident in their treatment of the executive. They would not have kept an institution that had characterized the proprietary government for seventy-five years if they had not been pleased with it.

It is hard to appraise the work of the single chamber in Pennsylvania during the years from 1776 to 1790. The general confusion of that period was aggravated in Pennsylvania by sharp conflict between political factions. The leading men of the state were moderate Whigs who would have none of the policies of the radical Constitutionalists that controlled the convention and affairs in the state thereafter. The moderates therefore withdrew from participation in the government. The sturdy Quaker stock also held aloof because most of them opposed the war with England. Consequently, the affairs of the state during this period were in the hands of mediocre men, for the most part, although Benjamin Franklin and Thomas Mifflin served as the last two presidents under the constitution of 1776.

Some of the criticism that developed was directed against the legislature and the council of censors, but most of it centered on the multiple executive. Many considered that device too democratic. It was unwieldy and its capacity, they said, was "only that of making trouble." The council of censors finally appointed a Committee on the Defects and Alterations of the Constitution. When the committee reported in 1784, it had this to say about the unicameral legislature:

Your committee, to whom it was referred to report those articles of the constitution which are defective and the alterations and amendments, begs leave to report,

That by the constitution of the State of Pennsylvania, the supreme legislative power is vested in one house of representatives, chosen by all those who pay public taxes. Your committee humbly conceives the said constitution to be in this respect materially defective:

1. Because if it should happen that a prevailing faction in that one house was desirous of enacting unjust and tyrannical laws, there is no check upon their proceedings.

2. Because an uncontrolled power of legislation will always enable the body possessing it, to usurp both the judicial and executive authority, in which case no remedy would remain to the people but by revolution.[24]

As a result of the general dissatisfaction, the control of the government soon passed from the Constitutionalists to the Federalists, who summoned a constitutional convention to meet in Philadelphia in November, 1789. The new con-

[24] Irma A. Watts, "Why Pennsylvania Abandoned Unicameralism," *State Government*, 9:54-55 (March, 1936).

stitution was adopted the following year. It set up the office of governor in place of the multiple executive; it abolished the council of censors; and it divided the legislature into two houses. Pennsylvania had joined the bicameral ranks.

Vermont. — The unicameral legislature of Vermont is worthy of treatment at more length for it lasted long enough (1777–1836) to make possible an estimate of its merits.[25] The constitutional convention of the Republic of Vermont assembled July 2 and completed its work July 8, 1777.[26] The constitution it produced was patterned largely on the Pennsylvania constitution of 1776. It assigned the "supreme executive powers" to an executive council, which included, in addition to the governor and the lieutenant governor, twelve persons elected by the voters of the state at large for a term of one year.[27] If the people should fail to give any candidate for governor or lieutenant governor a majority vote, the council and the legislature sitting together as a joint committee were to make the election.

The constitution further provided for a council of cen-

[25] Daniel Chipman, *A Memoir of Thomas Chittenden* (Middlebury, Vermont, 1849); Hiland Hall, *A History of Vermont from Its Discovery to Its Admission into the Union in 1791* (Albany, 1868); Nathan Hoskins, *A History of the State of Vermont* (Vergennes, Vermont, 1831).

[26] The first permanent settlement in the territory that now constitutes the state of Vermont was made at Bennington in 1761. This territory was claimed by New Hampshire, and the governor of New Hampshire conveyed to settlers what was known as the "New Hampshire Grants," consisting of 138 townships. New York also claimed the territory under a charter granted to the Duke of York by Charles II. An effort was made by Governor Tryon of New York to remove the settlers but under the leadership of such men as Ethan Allen and Seth Parker, the "Green Mountain Boys" declared their independence. A convention was called at which a constitution was framed, and members were selected to represent her in the Congress under the Confederacy. New York's opposition to Vermont's admission to the Confederacy prevented her from joining. It was not until 1791 that Vermont joined the Union as the fourteenth state, after satisfactory compensation, $30,000, had been made to satisfy New York's claim to Vermont's territory.

[27] For the constitution of Vermont and discussions of it, see Chipman, *A Memoir of Thomas Chittenden;* William Slade, compiler, *Vermont State Papers; Records and Documents* (Middlebury, Vermont, 1823), p. 241.

sors which was to serve as a general inquisitorial body to see that the constitution was preserved and that the legislative and executive branches of the government were properly performing their duties. It was given the exclusive power to propose amendments to the constitution and to call conventions to consider the amendments whenever two-thirds of its members should so agree. No member of the executive council or of the general assembly was eligible to a place on the council of censors.

The legislature was to be a single chamber called the General Assembly of the Representatives of the Freemen of Vermont. Its members were to be elected annually, and representation was based upon towns, each town to send one representative. The representatives were to choose their own speaker, secretary of state, and clerk. They were to determine their dates of adjournment, to be the judge of the election and qualifications of their own members, to bring charges of impeachment, to "prepare bills and enact them into laws," to grant charters of incorporation, and to have "all other powers necessary for the legislature of a free state." Such powers, however, were never to violate the constitution. The legislators were to originate and pass all laws, but before public bills could be enacted they had to be presented to the governor and council "for their perusal and proposals of amendment." From this exception apparently, there developed the conflict between the legislature and the executive council during which the latter gradually secured the right to act in an advisory capacity to the legislators, to impose a suspensive veto upon offending bills, and to initiate legislation.[28]

By far the most thorough and scholarly study which has yet been made of the unicameral legislature in Vermont is that by Professor Carroll.[29] According to his findings

[28] Hall, *A History of Vermont*, p. 269.
[29] Daniel B. Carroll, *The Unicameral Legislature of Vermont* (Montpelier, Vermont, 1933).

there seems to have been no special complaint about the unicameral legislature until just prior to the adoption of the bicameral system. Some even contended that the unicameral body was the most desirable feature of the constitution. The idea of changing to the bicameral system found its principal support in the council of censors, which repeatedly suggested amendments making the change. These were usually rejected by the conventions called to consider them. In 1792 the council's amendment received considerable support, though not enough for adoption. Professor Carroll accounts for this by explaining that the amendment also carried a provision to eliminate some of the inequalities in representation in the legislature. The feature of the amendment which interested the people, he contends, was not the adoption of a bicameral legislature, but the improvement in representation. Since the measures were combined, however, the people voted for the first in order to secure the second. There is little evidence that the people in general were interested in changing the form of government after 1792, and the newspapers make no mention of any such desire.

It was not until 1835 that a public sentiment developed over the election of a governor. As we have seen, when the governor failed to secure a majority vote, his election was thrown into a joint meeting of the council and the house of representatives. This situation materialized in 1835 and the duty of choosing the governor devolved upon the joint committee. There had developed within the state three political parties highly antagonistic to each other. Since the representation of the three parties in the house was very nearly equal, the committee spent twenty-four days trying to elect a governor. Without avail; the lieutenant governor had to serve during the unexpired term. Although the people had failed to elect a governor on several previous occasions, the joint committee had always before been able to secure an election. This experience gave the council of censors a timely argument to support their recommendations for a bicameral legislature. They could show that the present legislature had failed. Although no one knew how a legislature consisting of two chambers with equal powers would have solved the situation, the newspapers now joined the cry for a bicameral legislature.

Professor Carroll summarizes as follows the arguments advanced by the various councils of censors in their effort to secure the adoption of the bicameral system:

(a) That the tendency of the legislature toward hasty and unwise action would be checked, (b) that Vermont would be adopting a system which had been in successful operation in all of the states and in the United States for years, (c) that a more equitable distribution of representation in the legislative body of the state would be secured, (d) that the bicameral system would eliminate the "baneful effects of heat and party spirit," (e) that a shorter ballot would be secured if the bicameral system were adopted, (f) that the unicameral system was inherently vicious, (g) that the conflict between the Executive Council (Governor and Council) and the House of Representatives would be eliminated by the establishment of a senate, (h) that the superiority of the bicameral system had been proved by the experience of all ages, (i) that a simple form of governmental organization, such as that provided by the unicameral system, was not suited to a complex civilization, and (j) that the framers of the existing constitution had intended that the Executive Council have an absolute check upon, and complete equality with, the House of Representatives in the exercise of legislative authority and that this authority had recently been usurped by the House of Representatives.[30]

The proposal to replace the unicameral legislature with one of two chambers was adopted in a fairly close vote by the constitutional convention which met on January 6, 1836, just when the disappointment over the failure of the joint committee to elect a governor was at its height. The

[30] Carroll, *The Unicameral Legislature of Vermont*, pp. 26–27.

amendment provided for a governor who was to serve as the chief executive of the state. It abolished the council of censors but established in its place a senate of thirty members which was to have coordinate legislative powers with the house of representatives. The senators were to be apportioned among the counties according to population, though no county was to have less than one senator.

Irregularities in the passage of the amendment have been charged. It occurred at a time when there was developing throughout the country considerable agitation for the regulation of banks and other similar institutions, and there are some indications that certain business and financial interests gave active support to the change in favor of the bicameral system. These interests may also have influenced the newspapers to support the campaign in the fall of 1835 and later. There were irregularities in seating members at the constitutional convention too, and in spite of repeated efforts to call for the credentials on the charge that some had not been properly certified, the convention refused to consider the report of its committee on credentials.

Professor Carroll has made a study of the extent to which the claims set forth in favor of the senate were fulfilled after its establishment. He studied the legislation in Vermont for a ten-year period preceding the adoption of the bicameral system, and then for a period of ten years following its adoption. He also made a comparison of legislation under the bicameral system in New Hampshire for the ten-year period of 1826–35 with that enacted by the unicameral legislature in Vermont for the same period. His findings may be summarized briefly as follows:

(1) Neither system had any real advantage over the other in the age of the legislators.

(2) Laws passed by the unicameral legislature were more stable and were passed at a lower cost. This was true of both private and public laws. Furthermore, comparing the

laws passed in New Hampshire with those of Vermont for the same period gave the same results as were found in comparing the laws passed by Vermont in the two periods and under the two systems. Taking stability as the criterion for judging the quality of laws, that is, assuming that the better the law the fewer the changes needed, the laws enacted by the unicameral legislature of Vermont were clearly superior to those enacted by the bicameral legislature both in Vermont and in New Hampshire.

(3) Bills passed by one house and rejected by the other under the bicameral system in Vermont did not appear to be radically different from those that were enacted into law under the bicameral system, indicating that the checks as exercised by a second house, while operative to be sure, did not seem to have any direct bearing on the nature or quality of legislation defeated. There is no evidence that the action of the bicameral legislature was less hasty or less unwise than that of the unicameral body. What difference there was, if any, appears to lie in favor of the unicameral legislature.

(4) The inequality of representation in the legislative body was improved to some extent by the adoption of a senate whose membership was apportioned on the basis of population, but such an improvement might have been secured as well through a redistribution of seats in the unicameral legislature.

(5) There is no evidence to indicate that the bicameral system eliminated the "baneful effects of heat and party spirit," or that strife is inherent in the unicameral system.

(6) Instead of the shorter ballot anticipated, a longer ballot was actually the result, since the increased membership necessarily added to the number of people to be elected.

(7) It is difficult to see how the adoption of a senate served in any way to eliminate the conflict between the

executive council and the house of representatives, although the claim that it would do so was used as a pretext to secure the adoption of the bicameral system. To eliminate this friction, it would have been simpler to abolish the executive council without adding a second chamber.

As for the claims of the opposing side: "While the arguments of those who advocated the adoption of the bicameral system in Vermont do not stand up well under searching investigation, the contentions of the Vermont leaders who opposed the change — (a) that the people were happy and prosperous, satisfied with the existing scheme, and indignant because of the proposed change, (b) that the proposed change would eliminate the unicameral system, which was the best feature of the existing constitution, (c) that it would increase the cost of government and the tax burden of the people, (d) that it would lengthen the legislative sessions without giving any compensating benefit, (e) that it would remove the government farther from the people, and (f) that it was not necessary to have a scheme of governmental organization like that of other states — appear to be amply justified." [31] Professor Carroll concludes that:

A careful study of the nature of Vermont's unicameral legislature when in actual operation and of the results obtained by that institution for the people of the state in the light of the arguments that have been advanced in favor of unicameral legislatures generally and of Vermont's unicameral legislature in particular and in the light of the arguments that were advanced in favor of the bicameral system by leaders of Vermont has revealed much to support the advocates of the unicameral system and practically nothing to encourage the proponents of the bicameral scheme. [32]

But nonetheless, after Vermont adopted bicameralism, that system ruled without exception in the United States

[31] Carroll, *The Unicameral Legislature in Vermont*, p. 75.
[32] *Ibid.*, p. 70.

for just less than a hundred years. It became "so firmly rooted in the political thinking of the public" that two houses in the legislature came to be considered essential to the process of lawmaking. Usage and tradition made bicameralism an established institution in the United States, and one which there was a body of political philosophy and theory to support.

3

ARGUMENTS FOR AND AGAINST BICAMERALISM

THE THEORY SUPPORTING THE BICAMERAL SYSTEM

IT IS clear that the bicameral system originated and spread, not as a paper scheme logically and ideally conceived, but as a practical expedient adopted to achieve the very practical ends of one group or another in the conflicts we have outlined, Roundhead versus Cavalier and Conservative versus Liberal in England, Jacobin versus Royalist in France, and Federalist versus Anti-Federalist in the United States. As is often the case, the theory justifying the expedient developed after the system and not before it. It consists largely of the advantages to the general welfare that the protagonists in these conflicts claimed for the system in order to vindicate — and often to cloak — their personal or class motives.

Many political writers, including John Stuart Mill and William E. Lecky,[1] have contributed to the work of bringing these claims together and rounding them out into a reasoned, systematic defense of the bicameral system. Especially prominent among these writers are Chancellor Kent and Justice Story, whose commentaries comprehend most of the arguments for two chambers.[2] They indicted

[1] John Stuart Mill, *Representative Government* (New York, 1875); William E. Lecky, *Democracy and Liberty* (2 vols., New York, 1896).
[2] James Kent, *Commentaries on American Law* (14th ed., 4 vols., Boston,

the single house as an institution dominated by men who are rash, inconsiderate, oppressive, and subject to passions, intrigue, and the impulse of the moment. "The division of the legislature into two separate and independent branches," wrote Kent, "is founded on such obvious principles of good policy, and is so strongly recommended by the unequivocal language of experience, that it has obtained the general approbation of the people of this country." [3]

Although we have suggested some of the chief points in the theory supporting bicameralism in our account of the conflicts that gave it birth, it may be helpful to summarize the arguments even at the risk of repetition, for they constitute the main body of the bicameralist defense in the present controversy in the American states. Many of them are embodied in the general contention that the two-house organization provides a check on legislation, or as Bryce has phrased it, that "the chief advantage of dividing a legislature into two branches is that the one may check the haste and correct the mistakes of the other." [4] Breaking this argument into its component parts and adding those benefits it does not cover, we have the following advantages claimed for the bicameral system:

Bicameralism prevents hasty and careless legislation. It prevents measures from being hurriedly enacted into laws by interposing a period of delay between the passage of a bill in one house and its final adoption in the other. This interval provides for deliberation and possibly for an indication of public opinion on the matter. The independence of organization and personnel in a second house may also serve to check ill-advised measures. Either house may pass a

---

1896); Joseph Story, *Commentaries on the Constitution of the United States* (5th ed., 2 vols., Boston, 1891).

[3] *Commentaries on American Law*, vol. I, sec. 222.

[4] James Bryce, *The American Commonwealth* (3d ed., 2 vols., New York, 1893–95), 1:183.

grievous law, but the action of a second body, where the factors that influence the first one are absent, may prevent the final adoption of the bill. Unless due consideration and careful investigation prove the bill acceptable, it is likely to be defeated in the second house.

The second chamber provides a jealously critical review of legislation. This advantage is important enough to be listed separately although it is properly an explanatory point in the first argument. A second chamber is sure to look carefully for flaws in measures sent to it from the other house because it is invested with equal powers and is jealous of its prerogatives. It will guard closely against the adoption of legislation it considers undesirable. This check will be more effective when the memberships of the two chambers differ in viewpoint and interests. If a piece of legislation satisfies the requirements and meets the close scrutiny of two distinct bodies on guard against each other and representing different groups of the electorate, it is likely to be a necessary, or at least an inoffensive, measure. Moreover, the very fact that its bills must pass another body will make a legislative chamber more careful about both the content and the form of its measures. And "whatever naturally and necessarily awakens doubt, solicits caution, attracts inquiry, or stimulates vigilance and industry, is of value to aid us against precipitancy in framing or altering laws, as well as against yielding to the suggestions of indolence, the selfish projects of ambition, or the cunning devices of corrupt and hollow demagogues." [5] Chancellor Kent summarized this argument for a critical review when he wrote:

A hasty decision is not so likely to proceed to the solemnities of law when it is to be arrested in its course and made to undergo the deliberation and probably the jealous and critical revision of another and a rival body of men sitting in a different

[5] Story, *Commentaries on the Constitution,* pp. 408–09.

47

place and under better advantages to avoid the prepossessions and correct the errors of the other branch.[6]

A second chamber serves as a check against popular passions and impulses. It is declared to be a psychological fact that whatever interests or excites a number of separate individuals will, when they are brought together, interest or excite them still more. John Adams recognized this when he said, "A single assembly is liable to all the vices, follies, and frailties of an individual; subject to fits of humor, starts of passion, flights of enthusiasm, partialities or prejudice, and consequently productive of hasty results and absurd judgments."[7]

The bicameralist writers are agreed that legislation under such influences must be guarded against in representative assemblies, and that dividing the legislature into two houses is the way to do it. One of them says: "If parliamentary practice is a guarantee of liberty by excluding, in a high degree, impassioned legislation, and aiding in embodying, in the law, the collective mind of the legislature, the principle of two houses . . . is another and no less efficient guarantee."[8] And Kent maintained that the purpose of a second chamber was "to destroy the evil effects of sudden and strong excitement and of precipitate measures springing from passion, caprice, prejudices, personal influences, and party intrigue, which have been found by sad experience to exercise a potent and dangerous sway in single assemblies."[9]

This argument assumes, of course, a second chamber whose members are less influenced by the popular whim of the moment, are older perhaps, certainly more experienced in the science of lawmaking. This is more likely to

[6] *Commentaries on American Law,* vol. I, sec. 222.
[7] "Thoughts on Government," *Works of John Adams,* 4:195.
[8] Francis Lieber, *On Civil Liberty and Self Government* (3d ed., Philadelphia, 1875), p. 193.
[9] *Commentaries on American Law,* vol. I, sec. 222.

be the case if the members of the upper house are chosen for a longer term, represent a more conservative group, and form a council of "elder statesmen." Such a chamber acts as a stabilizing influence in legislative policy when the lower house tends to proceed too rapidly or to respond too quickly to a sudden fancy among the populace. In short, the second chamber ensures conservatism; it satisfies the desire for stability in government and quiets the fear of turmoil and experimentation. A recent writer has explained this function thus:

> The primary purpose of the legislature is to ascertain what the law ought to be; to determine, not what the will of the people commands, but what the reason of the people, the common consciousness, demands. The legislature must be so constructed as best to fulfill this purpose. Now the interpretation of the common consciousness is a far more difficult matter than the registry of the popular will. It requires research, reasoning, the balancing of opinions and interests, the classification of facts and the generalization of principles. A single body of men is always in danger of adopting hasty and one-sided views, of accepting facts upon insufficient tests, of being satisfied with incomplete generalizations, and mistaking happy phrases for sound principles. . . .
>
> A legislature of one chamber inclines too much to radicalism. One of three chambers or more would incline too much to conservatism. The true mean between conservatism and progress, and therefore the true interpretation of the common consciousness at each particular moment, will be best secured by the legislature of two chambers.[10]

Bicameralism is a deterrent to the usurpation of power by the legislature. A single chamber is in danger of becoming "avaricious," said John Adams, "and in time will not scruple to exempt itself from burdens, which it will lay, without compunction, upon its constituents. A single assembly is apt to grow ambitious, and after a time will not

[10] John W. Burgess, *Political Science and Comparative Constitutional Law* (2 vols., New York, 1910), 1:106–07. By permission of Ginn and Company, publishers.

hesitate to vote itself perpetual." [11] This danger of despotism in the single house has been a strong point with all the writers. John Stuart Mill feared the evils which might result "from the psychological effects of a recognition that a single chamber held the power to themselves and were not dependent upon any other body." He considered it important that no set of persons should be permitted, even temporarily, to make their will prevail in public affairs without having to ask the consent of someone else.[12] Lecky phrased his idea of the danger thus:

> Of all the forms of government that are possible among mankind I do not know any which is likely to be worse than the government of a single omnipotent democratic chamber. It is at least as susceptible as an individual despot to the temptations that grow out of the possession of an uncontrolled power, and it is likely to act with much less sense of responsibility and much less real deliberation.[13]

Chancellor Kent turned to history for examples of the usurpation of power by single chambers and pointed out the disasters that flowed from such unchecked power. He cited the example of the medieval Italian republics. They were single "unbalanced" assemblies and were "miserable failures." Similarly, the instability and violent measures of the National Convention in France, according to Kent, "continued for some years to fill all Europe with horror, and tended to display in a most forcible light, the misery of a single unchecked body of men, clothed with all the legislative powers of the state." [14]

Justice Story, too, felt that a second chamber provides the greatest security against encroachments upon the constitutional rights and liberties of the people. Every legislature tends to go beyond its proper bounds when there is

[11] *Works of John Adams*, 4:195.
[12] *Representative Government*, chap. 13.
[13] Lecky, *Democracy and Liberty*, 1:299.
[14] *Commentaries on American Law*, vol. I, sec. 222.

no constitutional authority to check its progress. Legislative powers are arbitrary at best, and when intrusted to a single chamber, they are potentially despotic. But if a second house exists to preserve the people's rights in the process of guarding its own position and powers, the first house will be less likely to attempt the invasion of constitutional rights. No better device has been found to safeguard the people against oppression than the creation of an "independent branch of censors to revise the legislative enactments of others." Historically, the second chamber has not always been entirely successful as a barrier to unconstitutional legislation, but it has served as an effective deterrent.

The two-chamber legislature likewise prevents the usurpation of powers by the executive, because its jealous guarding of its own position preserves the balance of power between the executive and legislative departments. At the same time it operates to maintain the independence of the executive, whereas a single chamber, elected by the people and feeling itself the sole representative of the popular will, tends to subject the executive to its control. Such a development, where it has occurred, has destroyed the balance between legislation and administration which the American tradition considers imperative for good government.[15]

A bicameral legislature is a security against the intrigues of scheming politicians and special-interest lobbies. "A job may have been smuggled through one house," said Bryce, "but the money needed to push it through the other may be wanting. Some wild scheme, professing to benefit the farmers, or the cattlemen, or the railroad employees, may, during its passage through the assembly, rouse enough attention from sensible people to enable them to stop it in

[15] J. C. Bluntchli, *Introduction to Political Science,* p. 434.

the Senate." [16] With two chambers in the legislature there is less opportunity for unscrupulous representatives to advance personal or party interests which are not for the common good, since the motives of greed or ambition for power are more likely to be detected when a measure must pass the double scrutiny of two separate bodies. The certainty of a second appraisal will discourage any effort to carry bills by surprise, intrigue, or corrupt party combinations. It is much less easy, says Story, to persuade two bodies into a "course subversive of the general good than it is one; especially if the elements of which they are composed are essentially different." [17]

The bicameral organization makes possible a division of the legislature's functions. It is the common practice to assign certain of the duties delegated to the legislature by the constitution to one house and others of them to the second house. In impeachment proceedings the lower house usually brings the charges and the upper house tries them to determine their truth. The lower house may initiate all bills for raising revenue, while the upper house passes upon the executive's appointments to office. Such a division of duties saves time and distributes power.

The bicameral system facilitates the adequate representation of all areas and groups. The possibility of granting representation in the two chambers on different bases is one of the principal arguments, or at least one of those most often used, in favor of bicameralism. Having two chambers makes possible the representation of different social classes, such as capital and labor or the aristocratic and democratic elements of the population, as in the English House of Lords and House of Commons. It makes possible the representation of political units in one chamber and the elected representatives of the people in the

[16] *The American Commonwealth*, 1:551.
[17] *Commentaries on the Constitution*, p. 400.

other, as in Germany before the World War. And it makes possible the representation of both population and geographical areas, as in our federal government. This so-called federal plan of representation has been used with good effect in several of the American states. We shall find an example of its advantages in California.[18] New Jersey, Rhode Island, Connecticut, South Carolina, and Montana also use it. In Montana the counties, and in Rhode Island the townships, are given equal representation in the senate, while representation in the lower house is based on population. In Connecticut representation in the senate is based on population and in the lower house on geographical areas.

Minority groups and areas of differing economic interests may also be given representation where there are two chambers and many representatives. For example, since the rise of cities with their concentration of population, the complaint is often made that representation according to population denies the rural areas of their proper share of legislators, that the voice of the farmers is being lost in the chorus of the city residents.[19] The bicameral system permits giving adequate representation to both these groups. Bluntchli stresses not only the advantage of giving representation to these various elements in the state but also the injustice of not giving it.[20] Moreover, where both the chambers have large memberships, the districts represented are small, so that the people can become better acquainted with their representative. They can discuss with him the issues of the moment and make him more aware of their interests and desires.

Bicameralism is the traditional type of legislature. It represents the "wisdom of past ages," the form determined by

[18] See below, pages 121–23.
[19] For further discussion and examples of this rural-urban conflict, see below, pages 65–66, 116–17, 121–23, 151.
[20] *Introduction to Political Science*, p. 434.

mankind through trial and error to be the most satisfactory legislative structure. History shows that liberal and democratic principles have invariably developed under governments having bicameral legislatures, governments where proper regard was given to the principle of checks and balances. The bicameral system has become so universally established that it has "become almost an axiom in political science that legislative bodies should consist of two chambers." [21] This argument, of course, has been of more importance in maintaining the bicameral system against threats of change than in securing its early adoption.[22]

CRITICISMS OF THE BICAMERAL SYSTEM IN PRACTICE

During recent years a mounting discontent with our legislative machinery and the laws it produces has come to challenge the validity of these theoretical arguments for bicameralism. The crescendo of criticism aroused by the inefficiency of our legislatures has put bicameralism on the defensive, and not only students of government but some legislators as well are asking whether the two-chamber legislature has the advantages in practice that have been claimed for it. A consideration of their criticisms is pertinent to our discussion.

The bicameral system does not guarantee time for careful deliberation on proposed legislation. This charge brings to mind the familiar and deplored end-of-the-session rush, marked by the hurried passage of many bills, some of which are known only by title to the members voting on them.

[21] J. W. Garner, *Introduction to Political Science* (New York, 1910), p. 436.

[22] Mr. Robert Luce, who served as a member of the Massachusetts legislature for many years, has written an interesting discussion of the advantages and disadvantages of the bicameral system (*Legislative Assemblies,* New York, 1934, pp. 3–64), in which he reaches the conclusion that the merits of that system outweigh its defects, at least as far as the Massachusetts legislature is concerned. It may be assumed that conditions in other legislatures are not so different as to limit the validity of his conclusion to Massachusetts.

David L. Colvin, in reporting his investigation of the New York legislature, says that in the closing weeks of the session of 1910 bills were piled two and three feet high on the members' desks.[23] During the last week 275 bills were voted on and 256 of them approved. Of these, 265 came up for consideration during the last four days, when other matters of business were being considered, so that the senators passed upon a total of four hundred bills, one hundred a day. Fully one-third of them had not been considered previously on the floor of the senate.

This was not an unusual occurrence, for the *New York Times* reported that in the 1929 session four hundred bills were disposed of on the last day, and Governor Roosevelt said of the 1931 rush, "I think that it is a fact that the legislature passed or killed more bills, many of them of a very important character, in the rush hours of the closing week, than they did in the whole previous three months of the session." [24]

Nor is New York just a black sheep among the states. On one occasion during the Ninety-first General Assembly of Ohio (1935) the senate passed fifty-one house bills in two hours. About the same degree of calm deliberation is indicated in the following description of the close of a session in Indiana:

One hundred and fifty laws were dumped on the desk of the governor during the last two days of the session. Prior to that time fewer than sixty had been sent to him. In the closing days, therefore, three-fourths of the legislation of the session was enacted, and in what horrible confusion! The last night of the session members could be found enrolling their own bills in any part of the capitol in order to get them signed by the presiding officer before adjournment. What a splendid chance to slip jokers into bills! What a splendid opportunity for the

---

[23] *The Bicameral Principle in the New York Legislature* (New York, 1913), p. 76.
[24] *The New York Times*, April 25, 1931, p. 6.

clever gentlemen who knew exactly what they wanted! In this confusion many good laws came through in such shape as to render them invalid.[25]

A former Colorado legislator describes a similar situation in his state:

On the day of adjournment, there is the inevitable accumulation of material which cannot be handled in a day. We work until midnight and then stop the clock. Sometimes we have continued on without sleep until the session was completed. In that case, the consequence is that the legislature may not adjourn until noon or afternoon of the following day — by which time most of the members are exhausted and somewhat dazed. Many of them are also highly temperamental, by this time, and some are quarrelsome.[26]

To which we might add that daze and exhaustion are not conducive to deliberation.

The New Mexico session of 1925 is another case in point. The senate discarded twenty-seven per cent of the ninety bills it acted on, but not one of those discarded was a measure of major importance. During the last three days of the session three bills were introduced in the senate by unanimous consent, the rules were suspended, and the bills were passed with unanimous votes. They were immediately sent to the house, where they were voted on without committee consideration. Two of them were again passed unanimously and the third received only two negative votes. The three bills were thus passed by both houses of the legislature and signed by the two presiding officers in not more than five hours — in spite of the fact that the constitution of New Mexico specifically requires three read-

[25] John A. Lapp, former legislative reference librarian in Indiana, quoted by Frederic A. Ogg and P. Orman Ray, *Introduction to American Government* (4th ed., New York, 1931), p. 716. By permission of the D. Appleton-Century Company, publishers.

[26] Senator Henry W. Toll in a letter, quoted in Joseph P. Chamberlain, *Legislative Processes: National and State* (New York, 1936), pp. 206–07. By permission of the D. Appleton-Century Company, publishers.

ings of a bill, not more than two of which are to be on the same day.

These three were not the only bills to be rushed through during that session. Nine others, all important and carrying total appropriations of more than $120,000, were rushed through the senate under suspended rules with unanimous votes. In the house, committees reported favorably on all of the bills except one, which was pigeon-holed. The other eight passed the house, five of them with unanimous votes.[27]

One more instance of this familiar evil was quoted from the *Topeka State Journal,* the official state paper of Kansas, by Governor George H. Hodges:

The bulk reading of omnibus appropriation bills totaling $1,318,779 was the only vaudeville feature of the day.

The Speaker announced "a bulk roll call and a bulk reading of bills"; and, calling a dozen owners of basso voices to the stand, each member was given a bill that carried an appropriation for some state institution or state department. "Is every one ready?" asked the Speaker. A dozen members, with a dozen bills, answered: "Aye, aye, sir!" "One for the money, two for the show, three to make ready — and four, they go!" shouted the presiding officer.

And the reading members went. They sang, and mumbled and shouted the words on the pages of the typewritten bills — each reading from a different bill, with separate provisions. "Louder!" shouted the members. "Louder! Louder!" chorused the gallery visitors, who saw a moment of revelry in an otherwise uneventful day.

While the bills were being read members pounded their desks and the reading ended in an uproar in which the members, clerks and visitors participated. The roll was called and a deliberative body of lawmakers placed its official approval on measures that called for the expenditure of one and a third million dollars, appropriated in bulk form, in a duration of possibly ten minutes of time.[28]

[27] John E. Hall, "The Bicameral Principle in the New Mexico Legislature," *National Municipal Review,* 16:185–90, 255–60 (March and April, 1927).

[28] "Common Sense for Commonwealths," *Saturday Evening Post,* 187:3 (June 12, 1915).

Fortunately, this Kansas incident is an extreme case, but it is only too certain that much legislative "deliberation" is done with equal celerity, if not with the same degree of levity. One is impelled to ask why. It is not entirely due to an incapacity for deliberation on the part of the legislators or to their human bent toward procrastination. It takes time to get the legislature organized, and time for the executive to study proposed measures and give his opinion on them. But the principal, and the most obvious, difficulty is the amount of legislation to be handled. In the California session of 1935 there were 3,636 bills introduced, excluding constitutional amendments and resolutions. Of these, 1,113 passed both houses and 853 became laws. No group could give adequate consideration to 853 bills. How then to 3,636? If a member of the New York assembly in 1910 had read all of the measures reported out of committee and all of the reprints made after amendment, he would have read nearly 2,000 bills — an obviously impossible task in the time allowed and in addition to the other duties of the legislator. Professor Paul S. Reinsch has commented on this situation as follows:

When it has become physically impossible for a legislator to give a careful reading to all the legislative bills proposed, even though he should use the entire time of the session, it is of course hopeless to expect the due consideration, weighing, and sifting of all the measures. Instead of fulfilling the ideal of rationally and thoroughly considering all proposed legislation, the work of the legislator ordinarily resolves itself to seeing that his own bills may receive a fair consideration, and to making such arrangements with other members that, by mutual assistance, their respective measures may have some chance of passage. In such arrangements the merits of individual bills are a minor consideration, the principal point being to ascertain what members are for the proposed measure and what they are able to do for other members in return for the assistance of the latter. It is therefore not surprising that our legislation should in general be haphazard, inconsistent, and often absolutely incompatible, and that there should be absent from it the effective correlation of new measures with the existing body of the law.[29]

These difficulties may not be due to the bicameral organization of the legislative body, but the fact remains that the two-house form is not securing the careful deliberation on legislation that its proponents have always claimed that it guaranteed.

A second chamber does not ensure a critical review of pending measures. This charge may seem redundant in the face of the facts we have cited; there can be no critical review when hundreds of bills are disposed of in a day or two. But aside from the question of time, how much of a check does the second house impose upon the legislation of the first? This was one of the questions considered by Dorothy Schaffter in her study of the functioning of six state legislatures. She found that in those states a larger proportion of bills introduced in the lower house were defeated by the lower house itself than by the senate, and that the lower house rejected more senate-initiated measures than the senators did bills originating in the lower house. She interprets this to mean that the lower houses were more critical and did more checking of proposed measures than the upper branches.[30] On the other hand, Colvin's study of the New York legislature showed that the senate defeated fourteen per cent of the bills passed by the lower house, whereas the latter checked only six per cent of those passed by the senate. The governor rejected more than either of them, vetoing twenty-five per cent of the laws sent to him.[31]

A similar analysis of the Wisconsin legislature showed that in that state the two houses discarded about the same proportion of measures, between thirteen and eighteen per

---

[29] *American Legislatures and Legislative Methods* (New York, 1913), p. 307. By permission of the D. Appleton-Century Company, publishers.

[30] *The Bicameral System in Practice* (Iowa City, 1929), pp. 108–09.

[31] Colvin, *The Bicameral Principle in the New York Legislature,* p. 83.

cent. In Illinois the lower house has discarded twice as many bills as has the senate, although in the years from 1907 to 1913 the two chambers exerted about the same amount of influence, each of them defeating approximately one in five of the bills sent to it from the other house.[32]

With these facts at hand, we cannot say that a second chamber fails entirely as a check on legislation. But it certainly is not so effective that it leaves no reason for dissatisfaction. The number of laws that have to be repealed or amended soon after their adoption shows the need for a much more critical appraisal of legislation while it is under consideration. From 1925 to 1929 the Pennsylvania legislature repealed 155 and amended 565 of the laws that had been passed in the preceding six years. In the Massachusetts legislative session of 1915, thirty per cent of the laws passed during the three preceding sessions were either amended or repealed. Such changes are usually needed to correct poor construction, incorrect facts, technical errors, or ambiguous provisions, although repeal may be necessary because the law was experimental in nature or was passed to meet temporary conditions. Even in these cases, however, the fault is commonly due to the failure of the legislature to consider suggested bills carefully, for a good experimental law cannot be adequately tested in a year or two, and circumstances seldom change rapidly enough to require a large-scale revision of laws a few years after their passage.

Further proof that the bicameral legislature does not furnish the necessary critical review is offered in the following statement:

[32] Finla Goff Crawford, *State Government* (New York, 1931), p. 119; for Illinois, also Walter F. Dodd, *State Government* (New York, 1928), pp. 143–46. Although many of these studies were made some years ago, Colvin's a quarter of a century ago, the congestion in our legislatures has grown as the problems confronting our lawmakers have become more numerous and more complex, so that conditions have probably not improved to the point of making the investigations valueless.

The veto messages of the governor constitute another possible test of the efficiency of the legislative process. An examination of the veto messages in Maryland and Pennsylvania for the regular sessions of 1927 and 1929 shows 51 laws in Maryland and 76 in Pennsylvania vetoed as unnecessary or as being duplications — in either case because similar laws were on the statute books covering the same subject; 12 laws in the first state and 34 in the second vetoed as being unconstitutional; 2 laws in Maryland and 19 in Pennsylvania vetoed as being contradictory to other laws enacted at the same session; and eleven vetoed in each state because of vague or careless wording. In the 1929 legislature in Pennsylvania, more than 100 laws were vetoed for the reason that they were technically defective.[33]

In those cases the critical review was given by the executive, and not by the second legislative chamber.

Why does the theory of critical revision not work? Some observers maintain that the very existence of two chambers makes probable a merely cursory appraisal of any bill, since each house assumes that the other has given or will give careful attention to the measure. According to the theory, the jealous rivalry between the houses will cause each to search for flaws in the laws passed by the other. That this does not appear in practice is probably due to a change which has taken place in the nature of the houses. The theory assumes that the two houses will differ in political point of view, in the social groups represented, and in age and experience. But today there is little distinction between the two houses in these respects.[34] More often than not their members are elected from the same districts, by the same people, and at the same election, so that there is little ground for jealousy or rivalry between them.

Where the houses differ in point of view today, it is a matter, not of social position, but of political partisanship.

[33] Clinton I. Winslow, *State Legislative Committees* (Baltimore, 1931), pp. 127–38.
[34] Since 1912, even the national Senate has been directly elected by the people instead of indirectly by the state legislatures, as it was originally.

That is a fact of great importance, for where both houses are of the same political party, there will be no conflict between them — and little "jealously critical revision" of each other's legislation. The second chamber will naturally give its approval to measures which the party leaders have sponsored in the first chamber. Even where the two houses are controlled by different parties, there may be harmony as long as no important issues are at stake. For example, in the New Mexico session of 1925, which we cited earlier,[35] the two houses were of opposing parties but concurred almost unanimously in the passage of bills during the close of the session.

But when party antagonisms are active, the "jealously critical revision" is likely to be carried to such an extreme that good measures are rejected along with the bad, and a deadlock results. There is no lack of examples of this situation. In 1912 there was a shift of parties in the election to the New York lower house, but the senate holdover produced a sharp conflict in the following session. As a result, almost none of the important legislation recommended by the governor in his annual message was enacted, only about one-half of the usual number of bills was passed, and little constructive work of any kind was accomplished. But the deadlock was not due to the rivalry between chambers as such; it was due to rivalry between political parties:

There was no pretense that one house was acting as a disinterested and sincere check on the other, no thought of one chamber being more capable than the other, no suspicion of one chamber being jealous of its own rights as a chamber against the other chamber. There was no idea of a conflict between the chambers, but it was a conflict between parties. It was the fact that one house was controlled by one party and the other by the other party which explained why little was done, and it would be ludicrous to attribute it to the inherent opposition of two formal chambers, or to any other cause asso-

[35] See above, pages 56–57.

ciated with the bicameral theory which failed to recognize the fact of diversity of parties.[36]

Much the same thing happened in the Ninety-first General Assembly of Ohio (1935). The senate was controlled by one party and the assembly by another. As a result, although that session lasted longer and cost the taxpayers more money than any other in the history of the state, it produced less constructive legislation than any other Ohio legislature during the past quarter of a century. There was said to be less cooperation and more antagonism between the two houses than at any other time in recent years.[37] The case for two chambers as a guaranty of critical revision for legislation may be summarized in the assertion that if both houses are of the same political complexion, one chamber is superfluous; if the two houses are controlled by different parties, the second house is likely to be obstructive.

We do not need two chambers to give representation to different elements in the population. There is some justification for the criticism that the two-chamber system is a relic of the days when governments recognized the special interests of social classes. The claim that facilitating the representation of different social classes and geographical areas is one of the chief advantages of the bicameral system undoubtedly developed in the early days of America's history. We have seen that the Federalists were such ardent defenders of the Senate primarily because they saw that it would afford representation to the wealthier, more aristocratic classes and would serve as a counterweight to the popular and democratic membership of the House of Representatives.[38]

But our legislative chambers no longer represent different social groups. There may be some difference in age,

[36] Colvin, *The Bicameral Principle in the New York Legislature*, p. 146.
[37] For a more detailed account of this Ohio session, see pages 109–13.
[38] See above, pages 27–30.

professional backgrounds, and legislative experience between the assembly and senate memberships, but often
there is little of even such variation. Suffrage qualifications
have been altered, and there is no longer a property requirement for voting because there are no recognized social
distinctions among the electors. Age, length of residence,
and citizenship are now, in most parts of the country, the
only limitations on the franchise. Most senators are elected
from the same district, by the same people, on the same
ballot, and at the same election as the representatives. It
would be hard today to defend the position that our bicameral legislatures offer any significant degree of representation to special social groups.

If there is no such differentiation of chambers, then many
of the arguments for bicameralism are without basis. If the
bicameral form means simply a duplication of lawmaking bodies, if one chamber is virtually the same as the
other in spite of slight differences in terms of office, if one
house is neither more conservative nor more radical than
the other, then bicameralism is merely a case of the state's
employing two identical groups to perform substantially
the same duties. That is needless — and costly — duplication.

As for affording representation to distinct geographical
areas or political units — that advantage of the bicameral
system was of real service in facilitating the compromise on
representation when the federal government was organized.[39] But we are not discussing the question of bicameralism in the federal government, where it is not yet under
fire apparently. In the state governments the question is
that of using counties and townships as bases for representation. Professor Finla G. Crawford has stated the issue and
pointed out the problem with which it is connected at
present:

[39] See above, pages 26–27.

If counties represent real economic and social units, the continuance of these areas as a basis for representation is justifiable. But on the other hand if county lines are artificial and historical, there is no justification for their retention. So much local pride has been developed in the years during which county lines have existed that it is well-nigh impossible to successfully propose their abolition as a basis for representation. For the immediate future, the county will no doubt endure and the result will be the continued existence of a rural-urban problem of representation in our state legislatures. Compromises may develop, but discriminations will exist.

The resident of the rural area maintains that the people of the cities should not control because of the vastly different social and economic structure of urban life. The reverse is equally true but the rural group is now in control and it is almost impossible to break its grip.[40]

Those last sentences touch on the one question of representation which is a real problem today: how to secure a fair distribution of representatives between populous urban centers and rural communities. The rural sections have claimed that representation on the basis of population alone gives predominance to the city voters. The bicameral organization was used to correct that, and several states have adopted the so-called federal plan of giving equal representation to all counties, or other units, in one of the legislative chambers. Now critics of bicameralism are pointing out that representation on such a basis is unfair to the urban communities.

California probably exemplifies this problem as well as any of the states. More than half the population of the state lives in the three counties of Alameda, Los Angeles, and San Francisco (including the city of that name). In a recent election of state senators these three counties cast 61 per cent of the total vote but elected only three senators. The rest of the state cast less than 39 per cent of the vote

[40] *State Government*, pp. 122–23. By permission of Henry Holt and Company, publishers.

but elected thirty-seven senators.[41] Since it requires the concurrence of at least twenty-two senators to vote an appropriation of state funds, the balance of power obviously rests with the rural communities. There are similar situations in many of the populous eastern states. In New Jersey eight counties with four-fifths of the population have eight senators, while thirteen counties with one-fifth of the population have thirteen senators. In Ohio twenty-nine rural counties with a combined population of 565,316 have twenty-nine representatives, while Hamilton County with a larger population (589,365) has only nine representatives.[42]

This certainly does not give fair representation to the populous urban districts, which contribute the major portion of the state's revenues. And it springs, the critics of bicameralism allege, from the very plan of dividing the legislature into two branches to afford representation to special groups, which the advocates of bicameralism claim as one of its chief advantages. Whatever its possibilities, the two-chambered legislature is not solving our major representation problem today. Whether or not another system could do so remains to be seen.

A large legislature is not an advantage. Membership in state senates ranges from 17 in Delaware, 18 in Utah, and 19 in Arizona to 51 in New York and Illinois and 67 in Minnesota. In assembly memberships the range is from 35 in Delaware and 51 in Arizona to 248 in Vermont, 262 in Connecticut, and 424 in New Hampshire. There is a natural tendency for state legislatures to increase in size because when a reapportionment of seats is made, it is more expedient politically to grant additional representa-

[41] Address of State Senator Walter McGovern before the Commonwealth Club of San Francisco. *The Commonwealth,* 12:222 (May 5, 1936).

[42] For a more detailed description of this situation in California, see below, pages 121–23. For further discussion of the same problem in Ohio, see below, pages 116–17.

tives to the districts that have gained in population than to reduce the number from those that have lost. It has been claimed that a large body of legislators is necessary for adequate representation of the electorate, but critics are pointing out that our legislatures are becoming unwieldy, that their size is slowing down the legislative processes. Senator George W. Norris of Nebraska has made the point that a large body is not truly representative because it must delegate its rights to smaller bodies.

One of the evils of our present legislatures is that they are entirely too large. In theory, a large legislature is supposed to give . . . a more complete representation of the entire citizenry. In practice, however, it has been demonstrated that a membership which is too large is detrimental to real representation of the people. A large body of men is not deliberative, and in order to accomplish any legislative results they must necessarily surrender many of their independent rights and prerogatives. In large bodies, members must deny themselves, in some degree at least, the right of debate, and even the right to make amendments. They must surrender to a smaller number of men or committees the right to determine procedure. The very size of the body sometimes makes it impossible for the necessary and proper discussion which should always take place before legislation is enacted into law.[43]

The size of the legislature not only destroys its efficiency as a deliberative body, but tends to increase its costs out of all proportion to its accomplishments. Additional members need additional employees and additional sinecures for their friends and relatives and political allies. Mulford Winsor, the state reference librarian of Arizona, asserts that "lack of responsibility, prevalence of the spoils system in its most wasteful form, and the irregular form of employment" contribute to make our present legislative output "absurdly expensive." Taxpayers have reason to complain of the mounting costs of legislation when there is no corre-

[43] "The Model Legislature," *Congressional Record,* 78:3276–80 (February 27, 1934).

sponding increase of efficiency or accomplishment. In spite of its sorry record, the session of the Ninety-first General Assembly of Ohio (1935) was the most expensive on record in that state; it cost one and a quarter million dollars.

Moreover, when numbers are high, salaries are proportionately lower; and lower salaries mean that only men of mediocre ability are attracted to the legislature. If the legislators are second-rate in caliber, the public will not, because it cannot, feel the respect for law and lawmakers that the citizenry of a democracy should.

It is the size of our legislatures, added to the amount of legislative business, that is largely responsible for the growth of the committee evil. Committees are necessary to handle the increasing traffic in laws crowding the legislative highways, but they often become participants in the jam rather than directing agencies to expedite movements of the traffic. That is largely because there are too many of them. The number in an assembly often reaches thirty and sometimes double that number. In 1917 the number of senate committees varied from five in Massachusetts and Wisconsin to sixty-two in Michigan, and in the lower house the numbers ranged from seven in Massachusetts to sixty-three in Kentucky and sixty-five in Michigan. Such a multiplication of committees as those upper ranges indicate places an impossible burden on committee members. Each legislator must serve on several committees and is often in a dilemma when two or three of them are meeting at the same time. The Citizens' League of Cleveland reports that during the 1935 session of the Ohio legislature members were seen wandering about the halls trying to decide which committee to attend and which to avoid. In one session of the Illinois legislature, some of the senators were members of thirty committees. Sometimes there are as many committees as there are members, in order to give each member the prestige of a committee chairmanship.

The absurdity of the situation is increased by a poor distribution of committee work. Some of the groups are overworked, while others have little or nothing to do. In the Ohio session of 1919, four house and four senate committees had no business to consider, while the senate judiciary committee was overwhelmed with eighty-two bills and the corresponding house committee with seventy-three. In the Illinois session of 1923 four committees received 454 of the 797 bills which the lower house referred to committees. Part of the trouble is that once a committee has been established, it continues to exist even though the purpose for which it was appointed has been accomplished. It is easier to continue a committee than it is to abolish it, perhaps because each of them carries with it the right to some secretarial assistance or some convenience like a separate office or telephone. Whatever the reasons, they cling like barnacles to the legislative hull.[44]

To the committees is delegated a large share of the legislative powers. In the Ohio session of 1935, which has furnished us with so many examples of modern legislative faults, 431 of the 905 bills introduced were killed in the committees to which they were referred; that is, they were never reported out for consideration on the floor. This is not an unusual occurrence, although in some states, such as Massachusetts and Wisconsin, no bill is considered disposed of until it has been voted on in one or both of the houses. In these states, all bills referred to a committee must be reported out again. The Ohio rules permit the legislature to call a bill forth from committee, but this is seldom done. To do it requires a petition signed by fifty per cent of the members and approved by the assembly, and the sentiment is so much in favor of the committee method that recourse to the petition is very rare.

[44] Winslow, *State Legislative Committees,* pp. 39, 42.

Critics charge that this method of defeating bills gives undemocratic powers to the committee members. In answer to the justifiable contention that many measures are introduced which are not worthy of consideration and should not be permitted to take up the time of the legislature as a whole, these critics raise the question, Who should pass upon the advisability of such measures? A small group of men controlled by a chairman who, in turn, may be controlled by individuals or organizations outside the legislature, or the entire assembly of elected representatives? They maintain that to acknowledge the inability of such an assembly to pass upon all the legislation proposed to it is to acknowledge the failure of the present legislative organization.

The committee system facilitates the domination of the assembly by party leaders or special-interest lobbies. It enables the speaker, for instance, to become a virtual dictator of the assembly, for he usually appoints the committees, and often has the added power of assigning bills to the respective committees. He can and often does use these powers to obstruct the passage of measures which are not approved by the party he represents. Lobbyists, too, find it easier to persuade a comparatively few committeemen to their way of thinking than to win the support of an entire assembly. That is why they find the large legislature, which works through numerous committees, easier to control than a small body which delegates fewer of its duties to special groups. Twenty-five years ago, Governor Hodges of Kansas pointed out that the two-house legislature remains a heavy and complicated mechanism, yielding readily enough to the political expert, but blocking at every turn the attempts of the people to work it. "Powerful private interests," he declared, "find their best shelter behind a multiplicity of barriers." [45] More recently a state senator of

[45] Quoted by Franklin Hichborn, writer and legislative correspondent,

California declared, "The two-house system is the lobbyists' paradise." [46] It is the delegation of power to committees that makes it so.

It can be argued with reason that although the committee evil is a modern legislative ill of serious degree, it is not inherent in, or peculiar to, the bicameral organization; but no one can deny that the existence of two chambers tends to double the number of committees if not their nuisance. There is one committee, however, and that the most troublesome of the lot, which is entirely the creature of the bicameral system. The conference committee with its wide powers results directly from the need for harmonizing the actions of the two chambers. When a bill is amended in the second chamber and the house in which it originated. refuses to concur in the amendment, the bill may be referred to a conference committee of members appointed by the presiding officers of the two houses. It is the committee's task to rephrase the measure or otherwise change it to a compromise form that will be acceptable to both houses. It may be restricted to a consideration of only those provisions of the measure that are at issue, or it may be permitted to reconsider the entire bill, depending on the rules of the particular state. When a majority of the committee has agreed on a compromise form, its report is made to both houses. If either house refuses to concur in the compromise, the measure is automatically dropped — unless it is referred back to conference with a new committee appointed to work on it. It can be debated but not amended by the chambers.

This sounds like a sensible procedure, and the conference committee is vigorously defended by many legislators, who maintain that it is simply a means of expediting legislation,

in an address before the Commonwealth Club of San Francisco. *The Commonwealth,* 12:229–30 (May 5, 1936).

[46] Walter McGovern, quoted in *The Commonwealth,* 12:221–22 (May 5, 1936).

and that action could not be concluded on some bills without it. The trouble lies in the possibilities of abuse, which are often realized to the full. Senator Norris has said that the conference committee is "in reality a third house" and "the most powerful of the three." [47] It is there that lobbyists and partisan politicians can exercise their strongest control, for the conference committee machinery is easily capable of manipulation. As a result, good measures, wanted by the public but not wanted by some special interest, may be defeated with apparently no one to blame.

The method of using the conference committee to avoid responsibility for scuttling a bill is quite simple. A desirable measure is amended in an unimportant particular by the second chamber to consider it. The first house is persuaded not to concur in the amendment and the bill goes to a conference committee. Appointed by the presiding officers of the two houses, the committee is probably composed of henchmen of those who are manipulating the procedure. The committee may, by agreement, be unable to reach a compromise, thereby killing the measure; or it may report the bill out of committee with important features dropped or undesirable ones added, and this mangled measure must either be accepted or rejected as it stands. The honest legislator's predicament in these circumstances is described in the following quotation from Senator Norris:

Whereas, of course, the very nature of the problems submitted to the committee requires a certain degree of compromise, it has often happened that the conference reports out a bill to which entirely new features have been added or from which the major issues in the two original bills have been eliminated. This conference committee report, which is then submitted to the legislature, must be accepted or rejected in entirety; it cannot be amended by either the house or the

[47] "Only One House," *State Government*, 7:209 (October, 1934). For statistics as to the role of conference committees in the Nebraska bicameral legislature, see below, pages 129–30.

senate. Thus the individual legislator must take what he believes to be bad in order to get what he believes to be good, or — if the bad seems to outweigh the good — he must vote for the defeat of the bill which he may sincerely believe has good potentialities.[48]

As an example, in the 1935 session of the California legislature everyone seemed to be agreed that a tax should be imposed on motor trucks using Diesel engines, for since they escape the gasoline tax, they do not contribute their share to the cost of maintaining the state's highways. But there was a difference of opinion as to the amount of tax that would be justifiable. A bill passed the assembly, the senate amended it, the assembly refused to concur, and the bill went to a conference committee, where it died when the legislature was adjourned. Who was responsible? That is the worst feature of such a procedure; the culprit or culprits are securely hidden. The public cannot know whom to hold responsible for the defeat or spoliation of the desired measure. Both houses have gone on record as favoring the bill, and since the sessions of the conference committee are secret and no record of how the members voted or minutes of their proceedings are kept, there is no way to assess the blame. The machinery of the conference committee provides the method par excellence for dodging responsibility. Everyone admits that the conference committee is a necessity under the bicameral system, but its reputation is so unsavory that the need for it tends to the discredit of the system rather than to the credit of the committee.

The bicameral system enables the legislator to escape responsibility. Critics charge that our present organization of government does not tend to develop responsible political leadership. Professor Buck says this is due partly to the bicameral system and partly to the principle of the

[48] *Ibid.*

separation of powers.[49] Under the bicameral system, responsibility for bad laws or for failure to support good ones cannot be fastened upon the individual senator or representative. A legislator may vote for a bill he does not approve because he expects it to be killed in the other house. There is sometimes even a prearranged agreement that the measure will be scuttled in the second chamber, or in a conference committee, as we have seen. This permits the legislator to maintain an unmerited prestige with his constituents by pointing to the fact that he supported the measure and helped to secure its passage in his own house.

Within the legislature, leadership devolves upon either the governor or the party boss, neither of whom can exercise open and responsible leadership. The governor is elected as the chief representative of his party in the state, but because of the separation of powers, he is often unable to direct proceedings in either house. His leadership must be indirect and behind the scenes, if it is to be at all. It will hardly be responsible under those circumstances. In the senate, policies are usually determined by an unofficial caucus of the party in control, and in the lower house it is the speaker who exercises the directive power. Where the same party holds a majority in both of the chambers, the senate caucus and the speaker of the house will both be under orders from the party boss, who may or may not be a member of the legislature. Where the two houses are controlled by rival parties, it is hard to secure constructive leadership of any kind. The legislature refuses to sanction the measures proposed by the governor and yet fails to provide leaders to institute a program of its own.

*   *   *

The existence of these defects, apparent to all, in our legislative machinery is destroying the confidence of the

[49] *Modernizing Our State Legislatures*, p. 10.

public in the lawmaking body, a development which is dangerous to representative government. But proposals for reform encounter inertia, vested interests, and a fundamental disagreement on the question of the bicameral system. Should it be maintained or discarded?

4

PROPOSED REMEDIES FOR
LEGISLATIVE ILLS

THE ideal legislature should be of "such outward structure and such internal organization as will render it an effective and responsible agency of the public will. It should not be of such size as to be unwieldy; nor should its form be such as needlessly to complicate the process of law-making, or to facilitate evading responsibility for what it enacts or fails to enact. Its internal organization and the rules governing its proceedings should be free from unnecessary complications, should seek to expedite work while yet giving each bill a fair opportunity to be considered, and should ensure full publicity for discussions, committee reports, and decisions. In the handling of financial legislation there should be close cooperation between those agencies of the government which are charged with raising the state's revenue and those which are authorized to appropriate and expend it. The lawmaking body should manifestly be composed of persons who are at least reasonably representative of the principal geographical sections and of the main social and economic groups within the state. It is indispensable, too, that they have the assistance of expert draftsmen, and that they be in a position to avail themselves of expert advice concerning the complicated problems which come before them.[1]

Few who are interested in the question of legislative reform would reject that description of the ideal legislature. The troublesome question is how best to achieve it. There

[1] Frederic A. Ogg and P. Orman Ray, *Essentials of American Government* (New York, 1936), p. 499. By permission of the D. Appleton-Century Company, publishers.

are many legislators and students of political science who feel that, in spite of its faults in practice, the traditional two-house legislature is inherently the best scheme of representative government yet devised. They advocate the adoption of reforms which would keep its basic features but would modernize and revise it to remove its disadvantages. Others scorn this as a mere patching process, which at best could be only partially effective. They maintain that the most logical way to remedy the present ills and to secure a better legislative product would be to discard the bicameral system entirely and adopt a single chamber in its stead.

REFORM WITHIN THE BICAMERAL SYSTEM

Reduction of size. — The plans for revision of the present system deal with three general problems: how to improve the quality of membership, how to improve the quality of legislation, and how to improve the rules of procedure. One obvious way of securing better legislators is to reduce the size of the legislature. This would make it possible, without increasing the costs, to pay high enough salaries to draw capable men into the work of lawmaking. At present business and professional men are almost excluded from state legislatures, not because of any legal restrictions but because the remuneration is not sufficient to compensate them for the loss of time from their business. Moreover, there is a limit to the number of first-rate minds available in a given area, and the memberships of many legislatures probably exceed that number. As Professor Beard suggests, "Not necessarily, but it seems to be safe to say that the larger the number, the narrower the horizon of the individual members. Men of capacious minds sometimes come from little districts, but the chances of securing persons of small caliber are increased by diminishing the size of the constituencies." [2]

[2] Charles A. Beard, *American Government and Politics* (New York, 1935), pp. 574–75. By permission of the Macmillan Company, publishers.

As we pointed out in the preceding chapter, this reduction in size would not decrease the deliberative or truly representative character of the legislature, rather the reverse.[3] Many students point out that a great number of city councils have reduced their memberships without arousing any serious complaint of lack of representation. And in the national House of Representatives there is one member for approximately every 300,000 in the population. Moreover, studies tend to show that the national Senate can dispose of its bills more rapidly than the larger House of Representatives and that consequently it often has to wait for measures to pass the more cumbersome body. We must conclude that the advantages of smaller memberships in our state legislatures could be secured without any serious loss. Nonetheless, the actual development has been in the opposite direction. Although during the last fifteen years two states have reduced the size of their senates, thirteen have increased it; and although five states have made slight reductions in the size of their lower houses, seventeen have added to it.

Longer terms. — Extending the term of office would be another way of improving the quality of membership. Two years is the customary length at present, but longer terms rotated so as to overlap would give permanency and stability to legislative programs and would increase the number of experienced legislators serving at any given time. A former senator in California proposes a six-year term with one-third of the members elected every two years.[4] Others propose a four-year term with half the membership elected biennially. In these plans the electorate is permitted to correct its mistakes in judgment by the use of the recall.

Direct primary. — Considerable attention has also been given to bettering election methods as a way of getting

[3] See above, page 67.
[4] Lewis L. Dennett, quoted in *The Commonwealth,* 12:248 (May 5, 1936).

abler and more responsible legislators. One method that has been tried is that of the direct primary instead of the party nomination of candidates. It was argued that when the party chose the candidates, mediocre men were selected because they would be more subservient to the party leaders. Experience with the direct primary has shown that, although it has gained some ground toward independence of action, it does not eliminate the partisan character of nominations and has achieved no spectacular reform.

Cumulative voting. — As early as 1870, Illinois adopted the plan of cumulative voting in the election of members to the lower house, in order to give minorities a representation which the plurality voting system did not allow them. Under this plan three representatives are elected from each district. The voter may ballot for three men or, if he prefers, cast three votes for one candidate. By bunching their votes, minority groups triple their strength and may elect their candidate. Although this reform in Illinois has not resulted in any marked improvement in the caliber of the representatives, it has provided a strong minority to counterbalance the tendency to corrupt practices which is present when one party maintains an overwhelming supremacy for an extended period.

Proportional representation. — Another plan now employed in a number of European countries and in a few American cities is that of proportional representation. To describe it briefly, this provides for large districts with a number of representatives from each. Votes are so counted that each party is represented in the legislature in proportion to its share of the total votes cast. For example, a party whose slate of candidates receives one-third of the votes cast in an election, is assigned one-third of the seats in the legislature. This assures representation to minority groups, but it sometimes results in no one party's having a working majority. In that case, it is necessary to resort to the bloc, or coalition of several parties, a device which is common in many European countries but which is not in much favor among American legislators.

Nonpartisan ballot. — The use of the nonpartisan ballot is another of the proposed election reforms. It has been in operation in Minnesota since 1913 and was made a feature of the election procedure for Nebraska's unicameral legislature. It has not eliminated party lines in Minnesota. Voters usually inform themselves as to the party affiliations of the candidates before they go to the polls, and the parties openly circulate their endorsements of the men they are supporting. At the close of the 1921 session, the governor so entirely forgot to observe the supposed nonpartisan character of the legislature that he publicly thanked the Republican members for their support of the party. The unavoidable conclusion is that the use of the nonpartisan ballot in Minnesota has only succeeded in destroying party responsibility. How it will work in Nebraska remains to be seen. Party lines appeared to be obliterated in her first unicameral legislature,[5] but much more observation and analysis are necessary before any final conclusion can be reached.

Limited sessions. — Several ways of improving the quality of legislation have been suggested. Since the quantity of bills to be passed upon is considered one of the principal causes of poor legislation, many advocates of reform have suggested limiting the number of laws. One of the simplest ways to do this is to shorten the length of the legislative sessions or to make them less frequent. Sixty days is usually suggested as the maximum length of session and biennial meetings as the ideal frequency. But these limitations will not work, at least in periods of emergency, as is shown by the numerous special sessions held throughout the depression. In 1933 forty-three special sessions were called in

[5] See below, pages 136–37, 143–44.

thirty-five states, and in 1935 every state legislature except Virginia's met either in regular or in special session, several sessions being necessary for some states.

Fewer private bills. — Since the majority of bills passed by the legislatures are of a private or local nature, steps have been taken to reduce the number of such laws to a minimum. One of the first methods tried was that of refusing a special act when there was a general law that covered the case. But this rule did not help much since the provision was permissive rather than mandatory and since the action of the legislature was not subject to judicial review. Missouri removed the difficulty by adopting a constitutional amendment permitting judicial review of the applicability of general laws. Other states have adopted constitutional restrictions which prohibit the legislature from passing special acts for such purposes as granting divorce, remitting fines, making changes in roads or in persons' names, granting changes of venue in civil and criminal cases, regulating township affairs, or granting special privileges to groups or individuals. Another plan requires that notice be sent to the communities involved before the special legislation is inaugurated and still another that, if the legislation involves a particular city, the approval of the mayor be secured. This latter plan was the basis for New York's "home rule provision," no longer in effect, which required applications for legislation for specific localities to come from the mayor to the governor, who then notified the legislature that an emergency existed. The special act required the concurrent action of two-thirds of both houses for adoption.

Initiative and referendum. — The use of the initiative and the referendum was hailed as a step forward in the movement for better legislation, and where these two devices have been adopted, they have exercised a beneficial influence. They permit the people to participate directly in lawmaking both by approving or rejecting measures passed by the legislature and by initiating measures which the legislature has not considered or has failed to pass. These methods of direct legislation are not in general use, for they have been instituted in only nineteen states. They have their disadvantages, too. If used often, they greatly increase the costs of legislation through the necessity for many special elections. They permit the passage of laws by a minority if the people at large are apathetic, and where they are used for constitutional amendments, they put the fundamental civil and political rights of minorities in the hands of a fickle, unstable majority.

Legislative council. — More concretely constructive is the recent trend toward the establishment of a legislative council as a means of giving coherence to the legislative program and curtailing the mass production of unimportant laws. Such a council is usually charged with the specific task of formulating a program to be submitted to the legislature at its regular session and with the general function of advising the legislators. It was first proposed in the model state constitution drawn up by the National Municipal League,[6] which provided for a unicameral legislature, but it has since been adapted to the bicameral system in several states. In Kansas and Michigan it is composed entirely of legislators, but in Wisconsin it is composed of a number of legislators appointed by the two houses and a like number of persons not connected with the legislature, who are appointed by the governor. The Wisconsin council centers around the executive. A similar agency in Colorado combines the governor and the leaders of the legislature.

The presence of legislators on such a council is considered indispensable because they have the advantage of experience in the legislature and can estimate the probable reaction to a measure on the floor of that body. This is an

[6] See below, pages 98–99.

important help in framing bills for presentation. The legislative councils also have the help of law and legislative reference bureaus and bill-drafting services in preparing bills in the proper legal form. The council usually meets between legislative sessions and draws up a program of the important measures to be considered at the next session. It pays special attention to the state government and to measures designed to increase its efficiency and to promote economy in its administration. Since, with the exception of the Kansas council, the members are not paid for their work, the councils generally do not spend much time in research on legislative projects. They act rather as revising agencies for the subcommittees appointed to study the various problems. The Kansas council managed, during its first year, to secure funds from private sources for the establishment of a research agency.

The recent formation of these legislative councils makes it impossible to estimate their value accurately. The one in Kansas seems to have accomplished the most, in spite of two defects that critics have pointed out; its membership (25) is too large, and it does not include the governor or any representative of the executive. At the conclusion of its first year's work, the director of its research agency wrote of it:

The Kansas experiment with a legislative council has probably made as much progress as could be expected under the circumstances, with the first year disrupted by special sessions and impeachment trials, and with no research staff until the last five months. While in certain aspects of the council's work little progress was made, in others the accomplishments were definitely of value and promise.[7]

Legislative reference bureau and bill-drafting service. — We spoke above of the legislative reference bureau and the bill-drafting service. These are two other proposed aids to

[7] Frederic H. Guild, "Achievements of the Kansas Legislative Council," *American Political Science Review,* 29:636 (August, 1935).

more intelligent legislation. They have been in the process of development for a number of years; the former has been established in about two-thirds of the states, the latter in only one-half of them. The function of the legislative reference bureau is to collect, and make available to the legislators, books, articles, editorials, and news statements that contain information or opinions relevant to the legislative problems. The bureau is usually in charge of a competent librarian, who catalogues the material under such appropriate topics as taxation, labor problems, and traffic regulation. The American Legislators' Association is making a valuable contribution to this service by facilitating the exchange of materials and by holding periodic conferences on problems of state government. There are also such private fact-finding organizations as the Brookings Institution in Washington and the Institute of Public Administration in New York, which provide technical studies on complex problems for the benefit of legislators.

The task of the legislative bill-drafting service is to aid the legislators by casting their laws in the proper legal form. The use of this service is not compulsory, but when it is used, it improves the quality of legislation by eliminating the technical defects and many of the ambiguities that otherwise cause so much difficulty. The bill-drafting service is operated in connection with the legislative reference bureau in those states where both these aids are maintained.

Executive assistance. — Legislative leaders are coming to rely more and more on executive advice and assistance in the preparation of bills, especially bills that have to do with state finances. In most states the governor is authorized to prepare the budget for the fiscal period and also to make recommendations concerning the legislative program at the beginning of the session. Some states also permit him to send messages on general matters to the legislature at any time during the session. In Minnesota bills cannot be introduced during the last twenty days of the session, that period being reserved to enable the governor to inaugurate important legislation that seems in danger of being overlooked. Massachusetts and New York grant their governors special powers over legislation in certain instances, thus making it possible for the executive to exert an effective leadership in the passage of measures near the close of the session.

Electric roll call. — Most of the attempts to improve legislative procedure are primarily concerned with the fixing of responsibility for legislation upon the proper house, group, or individual. Among these is the invention of the electric roll call, which was first put into operation in the lower house of the Wisconsin legislature and has since been installed by a number of states. It is a device equipped with a button on each member's desk, which is pressed to register the member's vote or failure to vote on a plainly visible board. To prevent an unauthorized person's casting the vote, each button is fitted with a lock and key. After all the votes are registered, the clerk holds the circuit open until anyone who wishes to change his vote has done so. Then the circuit is locked and a photograph of the vote is automatically taken to constitute a permanent record. This mechanism also enables legislators to vote simultaneously and without noise and confusion. When it was being recommended to the New York legislature, the proponents estimated that one-fifth of the legislature's time was spent in oral voting, and that the saving of time in one session alone would more than pay the cost of installation.[8]

The split session. — California's adoption of the split session in 1913 was also an attempt to make the legislators more responsible to the people. According to this plan the legislature convenes for thirty days, during which all bills to

[8] Arthur E. Buck, *Modernizing Our State Legislatures* (Philadelphia, 1936), p. 17.

be considered in the session are supposed to be introduced. Then the legislature recesses for thirty days to give both legislators and the public a chance to study the proposed measures. When the legislature reconvenes, its members discuss and act upon the bills, supposedly in accordance with their constituents' desires. The bills previously introduced may be amended, but no more bills may be introduced in either house except by the consent of three-fourths of the members, and in no case are more than two additional bills to be introduced by any one member. The plan has not proved very satisfactory in practice. It does not eliminate the rush at the end of the session; the recess is not long enough for any satisfactory examination of the ramifications and implications of the important bills; the recess gives lobbyists an opportunity to flood the state with propaganda in behalf of their interests; and legislators take advantage of their right to amend bills after the recess by introducing skeleton bills in the first part of the session and amending them during the second part until they lose all resemblance to their original form.[9]

Regulating the lobby. — The regulation of lobbyists has received considerable attention in suggestions for reform of legislative procedure. In most states congressional and legislative investigations have disclosed the evils of the lobby, and laws have been passed to curb its influence. Wisconsin and Massachusetts require lobbyists, or "legislative counsels," to register with the secretary of state, giving complete information as to employer, term of employment, and special interests involved. Some types of lobbying cannot be reached by such laws, such as social lobbying for instance, in which one is directed how to vote informally, at a banquet table perhaps, and one's social

---

[9] Massachusetts provided for a split session in its constitution, but its legislature has not attempted to use it. West Virginia adopted a similar plan in 1921 but abandoned it by constitutional amendment in 1928. For further discussion of the plan in California, see below, pages 120–21.

standing depends upon acquiescence with the suggestion. Nonetheless, laws like those in Wisconsin would help immeasurably to remove the most flagrant abuses of lobbying. For the lobbies that are open and aboveboard in their activities have real value. As one writer has pointed out,

It is now conceded the best informed persons, those most willing to impart information, and what is most important, to give it quickly in carefully prepared, well-marshalled, effective form, are the legislative agents of the interests concerned. Even though the data furnished must be rounded out and checked up from other sources to give a truthful, complete picture, many consider this to be the most important source of information at the legislator's disposal.[10]

The joint committee. — How to remedy the committee evil has been much discussed. The remedy is simple but not so easily effected. A reduction in the number of committees and a correlation of committee work are necessary. Reducing the number would permit members to devote their time to the more important committees and would thus increase the efficiency of committee action. As a means toward this end the joint committee has been suggested. Under this plan, which corresponds to the procedure in the Massachusetts legislature, bills are referred to joint committees of three or four members from the senate and eight to eleven members from the house. After consideration by this committee a bill is reported for action in both houses, which eliminates one committee stage. Another important feature of the Massachusetts plan is a public hearing on each bill, conducted by the committee at a day and hour announced in the official bulletin and in the newspapers. Bills must be reported out of the joint committee within a stated period and must be acted upon by the legislature before they are considered disposed of.[11]

[10] James T. Young, *The New American Government and Its Work* (New York, 1933), p. 505. By permission of the Macmillan Company, publishers.
[11] *Ibid.*

Correlation of committee work. — At present there is much unnecessary duplication in committee consideration because several groups may be working on different aspects of the same problem. For instance, the ways and means committee considers the raising of revenue and the appropriations committee deliberates on the spending of it. Such committees often engage in rivalry with each other instead of cooperating to solve a common problem. Reorganization of the committees to consolidate some of them and to correlate their programs would eliminate this difficulty, but as we have pointed out, the personal interests of committee members stand in the way of such an obvious solution.[12] California and Nebraska have tried to facilitate their committee work by preparing at the beginning of each session a definite schedule of committee meetings and hearings. The City Club of New York recommended that its state legislature require a written report on the merits of each bill considered in committee, the report to be a matter of public record and a copy of it to be furnished to each member of the legislature.

These are the reforms which advocates of bicameralism propose to make that system function effectively. Much more drastic than any of them, but steadily gaining adherents nonetheless, is the single-house legislature.

THE UNICAMERAL SYSTEM

The champions of the single house do not maintain that it alone is sufficient remedy for our legislative ills. They recognize the value of the other reforms we have described: they would make their single chamber small; they would furnish it with a legislative council, a legislative reference bureau, and an expert bill-drafting service; they would use longer, rotating terms and the nonpartisan ballot. Their

[12] See above, page 69.

contention is that adopting the one-house system is the most satisfactory, and probably the only possible, way of achieving these reforms. They point out that such a complete change of the legislative structure would provide a convenient occasion for the reorganization and consolidation of the standing committees, a much-needed reform that seems otherwise improbable. They declare that many of the present legislative difficulties, if not due to the bicameral system, have become so much a part of that system that to correct them is to abolish the system, in fact if not in name. If, for instance, it is necessary to institute a joint committee to reduce the surplus of committees, why not make the legislature frankly one body with one set of committees?

The case for unicameralism is present by implication in the arguments for and against bicameralism. The arguments for two houses imply those against one, and the arguments against two houses suggest those which support one. The points in favor of one house have been conveniently summarized in a statement issued by the Citizens' League of Cleveland:

It supplies a simpler, more direct, and more expeditious method of legislation.

It centralizes authority and fixes accountability, and therefore is more responsive to the public will.

It avoids the pitfalls, caused largely by the lobbies, which result in fatal delays and deadlocks between the two houses.

It is supported by the practical experience of American cities and the Canadian provinces.

It makes possible the development of leadership in legislation.

Its simplicity. — There are a number of telling arguments compressed into that first point. The advocates of unicameralism emphasize the fact that the simplicity of the single chamber is more in accord with recognized business practice. No one would think of having two sets of directors for the same corporation; why should confusion and duplication of effort be more justifiable in government than in business? In one small chamber, the lawmaking could be done with much more dispatch than at present, without sacrificing any thoroughness of consideration. There would be fewer members to take part in discussion and consequently more time for those who sponsor legislation to present its merits and for the opposition to disclose its defects.

Its economies. — The economy possible under the system is another strong point in its favor. Not only would the smaller membership reduce the total salary bill — even with higher salaries for more capable men — but savings in minor items such as transportation allowances, printing, postage, and clerical assistance would amount to a considerable sum. In speaking for the Nebraska amendment, Senator Norris said:

The plan outlined in the proposed amendment to the constitution would save money for the taxpayers. It would not only do away with many of the evils which now exist but the business of the state would be transacted at less cost. Many thousands of dollars would be saved annually to our taxpayers. The expense of the legislature is not only the salary that is paid to its members. There are hundreds of other items which enter into the expenses of a legislature, all of which increase as the membership increases.[13]

The possibility of accomplishing the same results more expeditiously and at less cost makes a strong appeal to a people who pay homage to efficiency. But the function of a legislature may not necessarily require efficiency. Perhaps that is better left to some other agency of the government which has a less specifically representative function. This idea is not a common one, but it is sufficiently worth thinking about that we quote at length an expression of it, which

---

[13] "The Model Legislature," *Congressional Record*, 78:3279 (February 27, 1934).

suggests an alternative to the unicameral legislature. It is an editorial comment from a California newspaper:

The *Sacramento Union,* impressed by the complete chaos of the present legislature and by the unanimous opinion of competent observers that this chaos is not the legislature's fault and is incurable under the present system, proposes as an alternative system, "a legislature consisting of one house limited to about thirty members, well paid and permitted to remain in session six months if necessary."

This is one form of a proposition frequently made by those who have observed the inherent inefficiency in all legislatures under the present system and who have also observed the efficiency which the commission form of government, with or without a city manager, has given to many city governments. We think, however, that the analogy is false and that the attempt to reorganize a legislature on mere considerations of efficiency would be likely to produce other evils even greater than those it cured. At least the experience of the world has shown that it is not necessary to make legislatures efficient in order to have government efficient. There is not an efficient legislature in the world, but there are many efficient governments. The remedy is not to make the legislature efficient, but to provide the efficiency from the executive department of government and to leave the legislature large enough to make it really representative of the people. Instead of the Union's single legislative house consisting of thirty members in session for six months, we might very well have a governor's cabinet of half or one-third this size, in session all the time. This cabinet, aside from its executive duties, could present to the legislature at the opening of its session matured legislative proposals, together with matured investigations and arguments thereupon. The legislature and its members would of course have also the right to present measures, but on matters affecting the whole state they would ordinarily be under no necessity for doing so. The chief task of the legislature would then be to discuss, amend and to pass or reject the measures proposed. For this purpose a large legislature, whether one house or two, directly representative of the people, would be better than a smaller house of professional governors. The responsibility of proposing legislation would be primarily on the governor and his cabinet, while the responsibility of deciding legislation would be on the legislature, as the people's representatives, or on the people themselves by referendum, whenever necessary.

At present this system is exactly reversed. The legislature proposes measures and the governor decides them, each department of government therefore undertaking the task for which it is least adapted and for which it was not elected. A democracy should provide for leadership as well as for representation and safety. If the governor and his cabinet were required to exert leadership and were held responsible for it and if the legislature and when necessary the people, were held primarily to the responsibility of passing upon the proposals presented by this leadership, it would be a more rationally democratic system. There would still remain to the people by initiative and to the legislature by its power to introduce bills the right to substitute unofficial leadership. As it is, the system works out nothing but confusion, and the only order that is put into it is done by the arbitrary power of the governor, after the legislature has adjourned.[14]

Strict accountability. — Unicameralists emphasize the fact that their plan would hold the legislator strictly accountable for his performance. There would be no convenient second chamber or conference committee to scuttle bills introduced merely for political prestige with constituents at home. There would still be the possibility of passing responsibility on to the governor, as is done in much of our present log-rolling, but it would be less easy to manage it with public attention focused on the activities of a small body. The representative would either conform to the wishes of his electors or would take the political consequences for disregarding them. If government that is responsive to the public will is what we want, the establishment of a unicameral legislature would be a long step toward our goal.

Checks to its power. — The principal charge against a single house is the old one of its potential despotism. Those

---

[14] Quoted in the *Sacramento Union*, April 22, 1919, from an editorial by Chester H. Rowell, which appeared in the *Fresno Republican*.

who oppose it argue that without a second chamber there would be no check on the legislators' power, no authority to censor their measures and check their encroachment on the people's constitutional rights. Friends of the plan answer that experience has shown that the check exerted by a second chamber is often only nominal, seldom results in good, and is occasionally detrimental to the public welfare. They point out that the executive veto, the use of the referendum and recall, and the privilege of resorting to state and federal courts for nullification of unconstitutional laws, which have proved to be more effective deterrents to unwise and unjust legislation, would still be available to restrain improper ambitions on the part of the legislature.

Its success in municipal government. — To the claim of bicameralists that the two-house form is traditional and that setting up one house would be a dangerous experiment with a long-untried arrangement, the unicameralists reply that the traditional bicameral structure has become obsolete and that unicameralism is a familiar plan in municipal government. They make much of the widespread use and comparative success of the single-chambered city council. The bicameral council was originally adopted "in more or less conscious imitation of the federal and state governments." [15] When Philadelphia established it in 1796, the fact that the largest city in America had adopted it "doubtless had much to do with the subsequent spread of the institution." [16] Gradually, however, the demand for a simpler and more responsible form of municipal government led to the spread of the unicameral council. By 1905 only ten of America's largest cities still had bicameral councils. By 1930 only one large city, New York, was left with one. "Today, not one of the twenty-five largest cities retains

[15] William Anderson, *American City Government* (New York, 1925), pp. 344–45.
[16] Thomas H. Reed, *Municipal Government in the United States* (New York, 1934), p. 69.

the bicameral council. Yet, in some of these cities, the single-chambered council not only represents more people than does many a state legislature, but also raises and appropriates more money and deals with important matters affecting the interest of more people than a considerable number of our state legislatures put together." [17] Although this municipal use of the one-chamber council has been developing over a long period of years, there is no sign of agitation for a return to the bicameral system. Except in a few habit-ruled localities in the south and east, bicameral councils "are considered mere anachronisms with no reason for being." [18]

The problem of legislative reform will be more easily and adequately solved if bicameralists and unicameralists will both keep in mind that antagonism between them is unnecessary. Both are seeking a remedy for legislative ills, and the one-house legislature is merely one, though the most drastic, of the measures proposed to that end. Whatever the plan adopted, it must be one that will effect "a renewal of confidence on the part of the people in the lawmaking body, which is essential to the maintenance of representative government."

[17] Ogg and Ray, *Introduction to American Government*, p. 688. By permission of the D. Appleton-Century Company, publishers.

[18] Anderson, *American City Government*, p. 345. For further facts on this subject, see Harry A. Barth, "Our City Councils," *National Municipal Review*, 13:294–99 (May, 1924); Howard White, "Can Legislatures Learn from City Councils," *American Political Science Review*, 21:95–100 (February, 1927).

5

THE INTEREST IN UNICAMERALISM
REVIVES

UNICAMERALISM is no longer merely an academic question. That is sufficiently clear from the number of amendments and resolutions which have lately been proposed toward the end of establishing single-chamber legislatures. The definite movement in that direction made its debut in 1912, when measures were introduced in two states, Ohio and Oregon. There has been scarcely a year since that time in which some such proposal was not being considered in one state or another, and the number brought forward each year has been increasing steadily. In 1931 and again in 1933 resolutions were introduced in some half a dozen states. Then in 1934 came Nebraska's adoption of the plan. Public interest rose sharply, and in 1935 more than a score of bills were proposed in approximately a dozen states. But even this record was broken in 1937. Some forty bills incorporating the one-house form were considered by twenty-one of the forty-three state legislatures in session that year, and three others appointed committees to study the question.[1] From 1935 to 1937 well over half the states had passed upon one or more measures designed to institute the unicameral system. That system has become a matter of general interest and practical significance.

[1] For the names of these states and the number and kind of proposal in each, see the table below, pages 152–55.

It is with these various proposals that we shall concern ourselves hereafter. We shall examine some of the earlier plans briefly and recent ones in Ohio and California, as well as the one adopted by Nebraska, at greater length. We shall conclude with a summary of the general tendencies discernible in a comparative study of the proposed plans.

Oregon. — The plan proposed in Oregon in 1912 was to abolish the senate, leaving the house of representatives as a single chamber of sixty members elected for a four-year term. It provided for closer cooperation between the legislative and executive departments by making the governor a member of the house and giving him the right to introduce all appropriation bills. An added feature, probably unique, was the provision that the defeated candidate for governor should also be given a seat in the legislature.

The amendment was submitted to the people and was defeated by more than 71,000 votes. But the fact that more than 30,000 ballots were cast in its favor shows an amount of approval that is surprising if we consider the weight of tradition, the special interests, and the prejudices that naturally oppose the unicameral system. The vote on a similar amendment submitted two years later was 62,376 for and 123,429 against.

Kansas. — It was Governor George H. Hodges who led the early agitation for legislative reform in Kansas. He was convinced that American state governments have become antiquated and cannot perform well the duties imposed upon the modern legislature. He argued for greater efficiency and a quicker response to the will of the people, which he felt unicameralism would provide. In 1913 Governor Hodges proposed to the Kansas legislators that they establish an assembly of from seven to sixteen members, elected from the congressional districts for a four- or six-year term. He recommended that the office of lieutenant governor be abolished and that the governor be an ex officio member and the presiding officer of the legislature. He favored frequent sessions for the assembly and salaries for the legislators sufficiently high to enable them to give all their time to the work of the government.[2] His speeches and writings aroused attention elsewhere as well as in Kansas.

Oklahoma. — In an election in 1914 the people of Oklahoma gave an affirmative vote to an amendment creating a one-house legislature. The measure, which had originated by use of the initiative, called for a chamber of eighty members. Of those who voted on the amendment, 99,686 were in favor and only 71,742 against. But it failed of adoption because it did not receive a majority of all the votes cast, which would have been 124,465.

Washington. — Between 1915 and 1920 a number of widely scattered states rejected unicameralist amendments. Alabama (1915), New York (1915), Arizona (1917), Massachusetts (1917), and Illinois (1920) were among them. Washington did not actually consider an amendment until much later, but Governor Ernest Lister, in his message to the legislature in 1915, expressed his conviction that better results in lawmaking would be secured in a smaller legislature of one house. He returned to the subject in his second inaugural message and urged that the state constitution be revised to make the legislature unicameral.

The resolution for which Governor Lister asked did not come until 1933.[3] Then it called for a chamber of twenty-four persons, four from each of the six congressional districts. The two members from each district who received the most votes were to serve for four years and the others for two years. The legislators were to elect the lieutenant governor and were to serve as heads of the various state

---

[2] For Governor Hodges' argument in favor of his plan, see his "Common Sense for Commonwealths," *Saturday Evening Post,* 187:3–6 (June 12, 1915).

[3] House Joint Resolution No. 5, 1933, introduced by Mr. Magnuson.

departments. Their salary was fixed at $467 per month. The governor was to preside over the legislative sessions, but he was to have no veto power. Although this plan was rejected by the people in a general election, the agitation for unicameralism has not died out in Washington. There were no less than six bills for a single-house legislature introduced during the 1937 session in that state.

South Dakota. — Interest in this question has been considerable in South Dakota. The legislative assemblies of 1917, 1919, 1923, 1925, 1927, and 1931, all considered some form of proposal for a unicameral body. Governor Norbeck presented the setting for this agitation when he said to the legislature of 1917:

There is considerable sentiment in favor of abolishing one legislative chamber. I think the idea is entirely practical. My experience as a member of the senate for several terms leads me to believe that the saving in expense is the least important item. The more important, I believe, is that it would result in better and more carefully considered laws where the responsibility was centered in one body. It is a common habit for one house to feel that if there is any error or any bad feature in a bill when it passes, the other house will surely look out for it. Each depends on the other and neither watches as closely as it should.

Most of the attention in South Dakota has centered on a plan which would give the single house fifteen members elected from nine judicial districts and three congressional districts. This body would meet in regular session four times a year. The members would give their whole time to government affairs and would receive from $3,500 to $5,000 annually.[4] A measure of this sort passed the South Dakota senate in 1925 but was rejected by the lower house. The governor urged reconsideration of the plan in 1927, but when a similar resolution was introduced in 1931, it was never reported out of committee.

Model state constitution of the National Municipal

[4] This is the plan proposed by State Senator Dowdell.

League. — Between the years 1919 and 1921, the Committee on State Government of the National Municipal League drafted a model state constitution, which provides for a unicameral legislature. Its members would be elected for two years by a system of proportional representation with a single transferable vote. The governor, elected for a four-year term, would appoint the heads of all executive departments, who would serve with him as members of the legislature. They would participate in the discussion of proposed measures but would not be permitted to vote on them. The governor would prepare the budget and would have the power to introduce bills.

Under this plan, the legislature would convene in regular session annually, or biennially, if so decided by law, and it could be summoned for special sessions by the governor or by a majority vote of the legislative council. For the plan would set up a legislative council, its personnel to include the governor and seven persons chosen by the legislature from its own members. This council would elect its own chairman and frame its own rules. Its duties would be to secure information concerning proposed or needed legislation and the general welfare of the state. In general, it would furnish guidance and leadership in the legislative program. Extra compensation would be provided for members of the legislative council in addition to their salaries as members of the legislature.

Wisconsin. — The interest in unicameralism in Wisconsin may be inferred from the fact that a constitutional amendment embodying it has been proposed at every regular session of the state legislature since 1927. Aside from the variation in the size of the chamber, from 12 to 133 members, the differences in these various proposals are not significant. The amendment of 1927 set up a chamber of 133 members, to be elected for four-year terms, one-half every two years.[5] The amendment of 1929 called for a much smaller chamber of one member from each congressional district (12).[6] The 1931 proposal reverted to the larger chamber, but the amendment of 1933 provided for a body of "not more than three members to each congressional district."[7] This would have made thirty-six the maximum membership. The legislators were to be elected for a four-year, rotating term. They were to meet biennially, but the governor or a majority of the legislators could call a special session. The salary for each member was to be fixed at $1,200 for a regular session; no extra remuneration, except a transportation allowance of ten cents a mile, was to be granted for special sessions. And "no stationery, newspapers, or other perquisites" were to be given to the legislators.

Minnesota. — Minnesota's interest in the question of a unicameral legislature has developed only recently. In 1935 the late Governor Floyd Olson said to the state legislature:

During past sessions of the legislature many members of those bodies have informed me that the work of the legislature is very difficult because of the excessive number of members in both houses. Accepting that as an existing fact, I hope I am not over-bold in suggesting to you that in a program of reduction in the agencies of government by you, your attention should first be directed toward reduction in the numbers of your own membership, and a redistricting of the legislative districts of Minnesota. I am heartily in favor of a unicameral legislature and I recommend that you submit a proposal to the people of the state for the establishment of that form of legislature, with a maximum membership.

In 1937 there were four amendments introduced proposing to create a unicameral assembly. This spurt of interest seems to be connected with the question of forcing

[5] Joint Resolution No. 17A, 1927, introduced by Mr. Coleman.
[6] Joint Resolution No. 131S, 1929, introduced by Senator Caldwell.
[7] Joint Resolution No. 48A, 1931, introduced by Mr. Wentz. Joint Resolution No. 26A, 1933, introduced by Mr. Weissleder.

a reduction in the size of the legislature. The Minnesota senate with its sixty-seven members has the unenviable distinction of being the largest upper house among state legislatures. The house of representatives is also large, having 131 members. Since the state constitution does not prescribe the number of legislators but merely fixes a maximum,[8] every reapportionment since 1860 has increased the number of legislators. The last reapportionment, in 1913, made the group three times its size in 1860.

Minnesota's legislature is also marked by a surplus of committees. The senate has forty-two standing committees.[9] Only four of these, the committees on aviation, military affairs, reapportionment, and the soldiers' home, have a membership of less than ten. The other senate committees range up to twenty-seven members. The fish committee has nineteen members; the finance committee, twenty-one; the taxes and tax laws committee, twenty-three; and the judiciary committee, twenty-seven. In the house of representatives there are forty-seven standing committees, which vary in size from five to thirty-seven members. The committee on engrossment and enrollment has five members; state parks, nine; corporations, eleven; rules, eleven; dairy products and livestock, twenty-five; judiciary, thirty; markets and marketing, thirty-one; appropriations, thirty-seven.

The size of these committees may not be out of proportion to the large size of the chambers in Minnesota, but it results in an overlapping of committee assignments and considerable difficulty in planning a schedule of committee meetings. The membership of many of these groups forms as large a body as some recent proposals suggest for the entire legislature. This results in confusion, delay, and poor work.

[8] Constitution of Minnesota, Article 4, Section 2.
[9] These figures are taken from the Minnesota Legislative Manual for 1937.

The committee evil and the tendency to become unwieldy are the two particular difficulties that have aroused
agitation for legislative reform in Minnesota. There have
been repeated attempts to reduce the size of the legislature,
but they have all failed. A bill to reduce the senate to 44
members and the house of representatives to 88 received
considerable support outside the legislature but little
within it. The legislators seem unwilling to vote themselves
out of a job. It is because these attempts have proved futile
that some Minnesotans have turned their attention to the
advantages of a unicameral house. But of the four amendments proposed in the 1937 session two failed to prescribe
any size or size range for the proposed chamber.[10] This
failure to guard against the evil they were designed to correct is certainly a weakness in these bills. The other two
measures set minimum and maximum numbers only, one
from 30 to 50 and the other from 131 to 145. The former
range is more in agreement with that in the majority of
the proposals introduced during the 1937 sessions.[11]

Since Minnesota has no serious problem of urban and
rural representation, all four proposals provide for districts
determined according to population. Only one of the bills
proposes a four-year term, the others specifying two years.
One bill omits any provision for the frequency of session
but the others call for biennial sessions, which is the custom
of the state's present bicameral legislature. One of the bills
would limit the length of the legislative session to ninety
days, which is Minnesota's current practice, although a bill
to remove the limit on regular sessions was introduced in
the 1937 session.

The demand felt in the state for longer regular sessions
is not urgent, but that for a smaller legislature is, and many

[10] For the numbers, sponsors, and provisions of these bills, see the table
below, pages 152–53.
[11] For a discussion of the general trend in the size of unicameral legislatures, see below, pages 149–50.

consider the adoption of a unicameral body the best way of satisfying that demand. The history of the state makes it clear that any attempt to reduce the size by a reapportionment bill would be useless. "Sentiment for the unicameral legislature plan seems to be strong in Minnesota," says a writer in the *Minneapolis Journal*. "The outlook is that if the idea gets before the people in the form of a constitutional amendment, it will carry. Whether or not it has the popular favor, it would seem that the voter ought to have the chance to accept or reject it." [12]

Arizona. — This youngest of the states has always shown a marked tendency toward adopting the latest developments in democratic government. The provision for the popular recall of judges which she incorporated in her state constitution was such an innovation that Congress frowned upon it and, at the suggestion of President Taft, refused to admit the state until the objectionable clause had been removed. Arizona obligingly struck it out, only to re-enact it after her admission. So it is not surprising to find that Arizona became one of the pioneer states in the movement for the simplification of legislative processes.

Governor Hunt's message to the legislature in 1915 called attention to the weaknesses of the bicameral structure and suggested the single chamber as a more economical and more efficient substitute. Little came of his words until 1917, when an amendment abolishing the state senate was proposed by the initiative and submitted to vote at the regular election of that year. It was sponsored by the State Federation of Labor, and although it could have been improved in form and was not adequately explained to the people, it secured 11,638 votes. Against it were 22,286.

In spite of this favorable showing, nothing more was done about the plan for several years. Other pressing needs

[12] Charles B. Cheney, "Minnesota Politics," *Minneapolis Journal*, February 18, 1937, p. 14.

and the lack of a proper organization and method for putting the matter before the people were contributing factors in the delay. In 1935 Governor Moeur joined the proponents of the new system and recommended its adoption to the legislature. Meanwhile Mr. Mulford Winsor had become the leader of the campaign for legislative reorganization. Having been the presiding officer of the state senate for three terms and being a student of legislative procedure with important studies of the unicameral system to his credit, Mr. Winsor is able to make his leadership authoritative and effective.

After a thorough investigation Mr. Winsor announced in 1932 that Arizona's legislature was suffering from a number of weaknesses, which he listed briefly as follows: (1) The legislative body is too large, and therefore unwieldy. (2) Its procedure is cumbersome and complicated, lending itself to corrupt parliamentary practices and hampering legitimate work. (3) The committee system is fatally defective and subject to many abuses; among other things, it prevents the public, and ofttimes the members, from knowing what is transpiring. (4) There is a serious lack of facilities for acquiring authentic information on legislative subjects. (5) The time limit on sessions imposes upon the legislature a harmful and dangerous pressure. (6) Under these conditions the legislature is not and cannot be a deliberative body in the full and correct meaning of the term. (7) There is no effective provision for the formulation of a constructive legislative program. (8) Lack of a practical plan of cooperation between the legislative and executive organs of government is a constant source of friction and misunderstanding, often resulting in disastrous deadlock. (9) The absence of any means, what with duplicate houses and multiple committees, of fixing definite responsibility for sins of commission or omission results in much dangerous legislation. (10) The legislative functions relating to public finance — appropriations and taxations — are not effectively coordinated. (11) The lack of a well-equipped technical staff results in mechanically faulty laws and opens the door to serious errors and more serious "jokers."

The plan of reorganization which Mr. Winsor proposes to remedy these difficulties would establish a legislature of one chamber supplemented by a legislative council. The chamber would be a small one of twenty-one members, to be known as delegates. The scheme of election would afford both geographical representation and representation according to population. It provides that one delegate shall be elected from each county, one additional delegate from each county casting "not less than 30,000 votes for the office of Governor at the last preceding regular election," and an additional delegate "for each 20,000 votes over and above 30,000." Enough delegates to make up the total of twenty-one would be elected from the state at large, with the condition that not more than five in all could be residents of a single county. The delegates would be elected for four-year terms, one-half of the number to be chosen every two years.

The plan sets no time limit for the legislative session; the legislature would convene annually and would remain in session until its business was concluded. In case of an emergency when the legislature was not in session, it could be summoned by the governor or by a majority vote of the legislative council. The governor and such other officers as might be designated by law would have seats in the legislative chamber. They would participate in the debate but would not vote. No bill could be passed until after an interval of forty-five legislative days from the time it was introduced. The governor's budget would have to be presented not later than the third Monday in February of each odd-numbered year; and following its presentation, no other measure could be considered until the budget bill had been disposed of, unless the governor requested the previous consideration of other specified matters.

Under this plan the legislature would be prohibited from establishing more than nine standing committees. The secretary of the legislature would have the right to appoint and supervise all employees of both the legislature and the legislative council, with such exceptions as might be determined by law. As for salaries, delegates elected from the counties would receive $2,400 a year, but delegates elected at large would receive $3,300. Mileage to and from the capital by the shortest route would be allowed the members but they could not collect for more than two trips a year. Other expenses incurred in the performance of duties authorized or directed by the legislature could also be allowed.

The legislative council looms large in this Arizona plan. It would have seven members: the president of the legislature, four legislative councilors elected biennially by the legislature from its own members, the governor, and an executive councilor chosen for an indefinite term by the governor, with regard to his "knowledge and skill in political science and state craft." When the legislature was in session, the legislative council could meet only with its consent; at other times the council would assemble of its own volition as its duties demanded. The president of the legislature would act as chairman of the council, and the council would appoint the secretary of the legislature, who would also act as ex officio secretary of the council. The councilors would designate the number of employees for both council and legislature and would determine their duties and their compensation.

But the council's principal duties would be those of a fact-finding committee, gathering available data concerning the government departments and institutions and concerning the general welfare of the state. The legislature would delegate to the council the power to pass judgment upon all primary relief bills, and it could delegate other such powers by law. The plan empowers the council to supplement legislation by ordinance, a provision which is not to be considered a delegation of legislative power. The amount of extra remuneration for the delegates who served as members of the legislative council would be determined by law. This plan also provides for the use of the initiative and the referendum and for a director of research, to be elected by the legislature to take charge of the legislative reference library.

Some of the virtues that its proponents claim for this comprehensive legislative machinery may be listed as follows: (1) The number of members would be permanently fixed, so that the legislature could not become unwieldy. (2) Representation would be equitable, both as to territory and as to population. (3) County-wide districts and delegateships-at-large would attract better-qualified men, so that the potential caliber of the legislative body would be improved. (4) The four-year term would give the legislators time to learn the business of lawmaking, and since only half the seats would be vacated at a time, more efficiency and continuity of purpose would be possible. (5) Machinery would be available for the formulation of an orderly, constructive legislative program, for securing authentic information, and for technical assistance in legislative procedures. (6) The absence of a time limit for the sessions would lessen pressure on the legislators, permit more careful consideration of measures proposed, and eliminate the evils of the last-hour rush. (7) Cooperation between the legislative and executive branches would be not only possible but necessary at many points. (8) Every legislative action would be a public one, and the fixing of responsibility would be facilitated.

The interest in the reform of Arizona's legislative structure is said to be growing, and the above plan has the support of many of the legislators themselves. But the evils inherent in the bicameral system are likely to prevent the legislature from taking action. The amendment to provide for a unicameral assembly may have to originate in the initiative.[13]

[13] Unicameralist amendments were also proposed and rejected in New York (1936), Massachusetts (1936), Maine (1935), Missouri (1935), and Utah (1935) . When the New York Bureau of Municipal Research made a governmental survey of Nevada in 1924, it recommended a one-chamber legislature for that state. *Nevada State Journal,* November 20, 1924; *National Municipal Review,* 14:679 (1925).

6

OHIO AND CALIFORNIA STUDY PLANS
FOR A UNICAMERAL LEGISLATURE

OHIO

THE performance of the Ninety-first General Assembly of Ohio (1935) gave an impetus to the movement for legislative reorganization in that state. It roused the ire of Ohioans because it was "the worst General Assembly at a time when the state needed the best." The Citizens' League of Cleveland charged it with establishing four unenviable records: it lasted longer, cost more, accomplished less, and wrangled oftener than any other legislature in the history of the state.[1] It was in session for nearly five months, but practically nothing was accomplished during the first four weeks. When the assembly first convened, the party groups chose their leaders in both houses and then adjourned for an entire week, leaving the formulation of organization and plans to these leaders. It was more than three weeks before the speaker announced the committees and another week before they were organized. A month had passed before the old rules of procedure were adopted. Members had spent the time largely in seeking committee chairmanships and jobs for political friends.

[1] This account of the Ninety-first General Assembly is based largely on the report of the State Committee of the Citizens' League of Cleveland. This league is a nonpartisan association organized for the promotion of honest government in Cleveland and Cuyahoga County. Mr. Mayo Fesler is its director.

Continued procrastination marked the next three and a half months. The assembly indulged in repeated recesses and adjournments and even when in session did little toward disposing of the legislation before it. As a result it had to act upon its important legislation, largely without discussion or deliberation, in the last three or four weeks of the session. Some idea of its last-minute rush to clear the calendars may be gathered from the fact that during the last legislative day, which was extended by the usual tampering with the clock, action of some sort was taken on 153 of the 391 bills considered by the lower house during the entire session.

State	Session	Total Costs
Michigan	1935–36	$ 461,919.00
Wisconsin	1935–36	321,178.67
California	1933–34	701,460.56
Indiana	1934–35	162,276.16
Virginia	1934–35	257,613.00
Ohio	1935–36	1,250,000.00*

* Approximate.

All of this delay was expensive. The legislature was costing the taxpayers $12,000 a day, to say nothing of the waste of public funds involved in the distribution of sinecures to political allies. The Ohio legislature paid more than $228,000 for the services of such employees as clerks, stenographers, doorkeepers, cloak-room attendants, and maids, which was twice as much as the Wisconsin legislature paid for such help in the same year. This item of expense has increased nearly four times in Ohio in the last eight years, and there has been a similar increase in the total cost of the session. The session of 1929 cost $626,894.28; that of 1931, $781,152.38; that of 1933, $910,119.54; and that of 1935, approximately $1,250,000.00 (this is not the total because not all of the charges were in when the compilation was made). The above table of costs shows how the totals in Ohio compare with those in other states.

In spite of the time and money spent, the assembly accomplished little. During the session there were 459 measures introduced in the senate and 697 in the house, making a grand total of 1,156. Of these, 905 were bills and 251 were resolutions. The latter were largely of routine character and were disposed of with some expedition; "but in the handling of the bills introduced, the legislative machinery creaked almost to a standstill, and resumed its motion only during the last weeks of the session when action at any price was imperative on certain measures." Of the 905 bills introduced, 514 were never considered on the floor of the house where they originated, 431 dying in committee and 58 on the calendar; 12 were returned to their authors; 4 received no material action after being reported out of the committee; and 9 saw no action of any sort after their introduction, except one, which was read a second time and ordered to be printed. Only 391 of the 905 bills were considered by the entire membership of the house in which they were introduced. A complete summary of the disposition of the proposed bills is given in the following tabulation, taken from the report of the State Committee of the Citizens' League:

Fate of Bills	Total	Senate	House
Introduced	905	351	554
Sent to committee	876	345	531
Reported out of committee	445	187	258*
Died in committee	431	158	273†
Not sent to committee	29	6	23
Returned to author	12	0	12
No material action after introduction	9	0	9
Acted upon	8	6	2
Bills killed by miscellaneous action	90	36	54
Recommitted to committee	8	5	3

* Includes three bills taken from committee but not acted upon.
† Includes one bill taken from committee but not acted upon.

Fate of Bills	Total	Senate	House
No material action after committee's report	4	2	2
Died on calendar	58	27	31
Tabled, postponed, etc.	20	2	18‡
Voted on by house where introduced	363	157	206
Passed	350	155	195
Defeated	13	2	11
Passed but not sent to other house	1	0	1
Received in other house	349	155	194
Sent to committee in other house	323	143	180
Reported out of committee	268	114	154
Died in committee	55	29	26
Not sent to committee in other house	26	12	14**
Returned to first house	1	1	0
No material action after receipt of bill	10	2	8
Acted upon	15	9	6
Bills killed in other house by miscellaneous action	44	18	26
Recommitted to committee	4	2	2
No material action after committee report	1	1	0
Died on calendar	38	14	24
Tabled, postponed, etc.	1	1	0
Voted on by other house	239	105	134
Passed	230	96	134
Defeated	9	9	0
Died due to failure to agree on amendments	2	1	1
Sent to governor	228	95	133
Approved	1	1	0
Law without signature	12	9	3
Vetoed	0	0	0
Passed over veto	0	0	0
Total laws enacted	216	86	130

‡ Includes two bills passed, then reconsidered and tabled.
** Includes one bill taken from committee and acted upon.

The discreditable performance of this assembly was partly due to the fact that the two houses were controlled by different political parties. The Democrats had a majority of six in the senate, while the Republicans had a majority of one in the house. But there was also a "hopeless incapacity to work with any degree of efficiency," which was seemingly inherent in the organization and procedure of the body. Instead of revising its rules, it clung tenaciously to old ones, many of which were obsolete. This was particularly true of the lower house, but the reorganization undertaken by the senate amounted to very little. The assembly was also grievously overburdened with committees, and they, at the mercy of their chairmen, frequently delayed their consideration of the measures referred to them. In short, the State Committee of the Citizens' League declares that every defect which authorities attribute to the two-house system was present in the Ninety-first General Assembly of Ohio.

The committee summarizes these defects as follows: (1) The two-house system increases the cost of the lawmaking machinery. (2) It encourages log-rolling and compromise. Scarcely one piece of important legislation was enacted in the Ohio assembly without sacrificing principle to expediency in the maneuvering between the two houses. (3) It affords countless opportunities for obstruction and delay. The many important measures lying in committee morgue at the end of the session are a proof of this defect. (4) It affords a fertile field for the special-interest lobbies. Never in Ohio's history were these lobbies more effective in defeating needed legislation. (5) It makes wise legislative planning impossible. The best illustration of this defect is the inability of the two houses to work out any satisfactory program of relief measures. What one house was for the other was against.[2]

This situation has convinced the Citizens' League that it is time "for the people of Ohio to consider some basic reforms in the legislative branch with a view to removing these fatal defects in the present organization of the Gen-

[2] For further discussion of the inability of the Ohio legislature to deal effectively with the problems that confront it, see Stephen Johnson, "Ohio Legislature," *Law Journal of the Student Bar*, vol. 1, no. 2. This journal is published at Ohio State University.

eral Assembly; and to create a legislative body which will really function and be responsive to the public will." The "basic reform" proposed by the league is a one-house legislature, which it considers the only possible solution for the problem, "just as the one-house council was found to be essential to the solution of the legislative difficulties in our cities."

Unicameralism was not a new idea in the state. Ohio had joined the van of the movement by considering a unicameralist amendment in 1912. The amendment was rejected, and there was no further activity in that direction until 1934, when the Ohio Chamber of Commerce proposed that the state adopt a one-house legislature of about fifty members. The movement came to real life during the 1937 legislative session, when five bills were introduced proposing a one-house reorganization of the legislature.[3] House Joint Resolution No. 10 called for biennial elections of the legislators by the "electors of the respective counties," but it did not prescribe either the size of the assembly or the salary to be paid the members. House Joint Resolution No. 11 provided for two classes of representatives, the one to be elected from the counties biennially and to receive a salary of $3,600, the other to be elected from the districts for a four-year term and to be paid $6,000. It declared any person having a financial interest in any business concern ineligible for election as a district representative. House Joint Resolution No. 16 provided for an assembly of eighty members to be elected biennially from single-member districts apportioned according to population. It provided for a virtually continuous session by forbidding a recess of more than three months' duration.

[3] House Joint Resolution No. 10, introduced by Mr. Thorne; House Joint Resolution No. 11, introduced by Mr. Kasch; House Joint Resolution No. 16, introduced by Mr. Harter; House Joint Resolution No. 26, introduced by Mr. Hudlett; and House Joint Resolution No. 59, introduced by Messrs. Doyle, Harter, Huml, and Hudlett.

House Joint Resolution No. 26 was the amendment proposed by the Citizens' League of Cleveland. If adopted, this plan would vest the legislative power in a single chamber composed of twenty-four senators and eighty representatives, but it would reserve to the people the right to propose and to approve or reject both laws and amendments through the use of the initiative and referendum. The senators would be elected quadrennially and the representatives biennially. The assembly would convene annually, with special sessions to be called by the governor or by the speaker upon a petition signed by two-thirds of the legislators, providing thirty days had elapsed since the last adjournment or recess. The governor and administrative department heads would have seats in the legislature. They could participate in the discussions but could not vote. The lieutenant governor would act as the speaker of the assembly and also as chairman of the legislative council.

Because of the part it assigns to the legislative council, this Citizens' League plan has been called a modification of the unicameral system. An examination of the council's duties, however, shows that it would in no way function as a second legislative chamber. The senators would constitute its personnel. They would meet once a month, or at such other intervals as might be required by law or by the rules of the council, both during and between the legislative sessions. They would conduct investigations on matters relevant to state and local government, advise the governor in the formulation of administrative policies, make recommendations concerning appropriations, propose measures to be submitted to the general assembly, and perform such other duties incident to legislation as might be provided by law. The secretary of the council would serve as clerk or secretary of the assembly and also as director of the legislative reference bureau provided for in the plan.

The amount of the salaries for the members and officers of the assembly would be determined by law, with the proviso that the salaries of senators be kept double that of representatives. In addition the legislators would be allowed "actual traveling expenses" incurred in "going once and returning once each week by the shortest routes to and from their homes" — this allowance to apply only when the assembly was in session and the legislator concerned had been in attendance. Members of the legislative council would also be allowed compensation for expenses incurred in connection with their official duties.

One of the major problems to be solved in any successful reorganization of the Ohio legislature is that of apportioning the representation of rural and urban counties. Under the present arrangement in that state, every county, however small, is entitled to one member in the house of representatives, although the prescribed unit of representation is 66,466.[4] This means that such counties as Vinton and Geauga have each a representative for approximately 15,000 persons, while Cuyahoga County also has only one representative for its 66,500 residents. There are twenty-nine counties in Ohio with less than 25,000 population, each of which has one representative; there are twenty-seven other counties with populations of 40,000 to 80,000, each of which also has only one representative. Twenty-nine rural counties with a combined population of 565,316 have twenty-nine representatives, while Hamilton County with the larger population of 589,365 has only nine representatives. Voters living in Hamilton County, therefore, have less than one-third as much voice in the state house of representatives as their neighbors in the rural counties. Sixty-four rural counties with a combined population of 1,781,282 have sixty-four representatives, while eleven urban counties with a total population twice as large

[4] Constitution of Ohio (1903), Article 11, Section 2.

(3,921,466) have only thirty-eight representatives. This manifestly gives the rural areas undue weight in legislation.

Naturally, the rural residents, afraid of losing this preponderance, are inclined to oppose any plan for reorganizing the legislature. On the other hand, although some in the urban communities insist on representation strictly according to population, others realize that a large block of members from a populous county frequently has more weight in legislation than the number in the block would lead one to expect. These observers propose a compromise which would divide the total number of representatives equally between rural and urban counties.

The league's proposed amendment incorporates this compromise solution of the problem. It would establish a board of apportionment, to consist of the governor, the auditor, the secretary of state, and two laymen appointed by the three officials, with the provision that no more than three shall be members of the same political party. This board would apportion the assembly districts by dividing the counties into two groups and redividing each group into districts.[5] The first group would include all counties with a population of more than 200,000; the second group would include all other counties in the state. The amendment provides: "Each group shall be entitled to one-half of the total number of representatives. The total population in each group of counties shall be divided by the number forty (40), and the quotient shall be the ratio of representation in each group until changed, following the next federal census." This apportionment would still allow the rural communities an advantage, but it would remove the conspicuous inequalities that exist at present.

The fifth of the 1937 proposals, House Joint Resolution

[5] Inequalities have also developed in the congressional districts since they were last redrawn in 1913, and the board of apportionment would establish new ones by dividing the state into as many equally populated sections as Ohio has representatives in the national Congress.

No. 59, is the amendment proposed by the Ohio Single-House Legislature League, an organization supported by the Scripps-Howard papers and other newspapers in the state.[6] This amendment provides for a single chamber of approximately one hundred members, who would be elected from single-member districts established by the assembly so as to comprise contiguous territory and contain approximately equal populations. Reapportionments would be made every ten years. Members would take office on the first day of January following the adoption of the amendment and would serve for two years. Their salaries would be determined by law and would be paid in equal monthly installments. No member of the assembly would be eligible for appointment to state offices during his term or for one year thereafter.

This plan would make the lieutenant governor the presiding officer of the legislature. It would not give the governor a seat in the legislature but would give him his usual veto power. Since the amendment retains the partisan ballot, the governor would probably furnish the political leadership. The amendment would establish a legislative council of not more than fifteen members elected by the assembly from its own membership. This council would make its investigations and perform its duties under the direction and control of the assembly. The amendment authorizes the assembly to provide additional salaries for the council members and to reimburse them for their actual traveling expenses while engaged in official business.

The amendment attempts to assure the fixing of responsibility by providing that the names of those voting for and against a measure must be entered on the journal if such a record is requested by any member. A record vote would be required for the engrossment of a bill, and except in

[6] Mr. Norman H. Ford is the league's secretary, and its headquarters are at 18 Parsons Avenue, Columbus, Ohio.

the case of emergency measures, no bill could come up for final passage until ten days after it had been engrossed. A second record vote would be required for adoption.

This amendment is receiving considerable support in Ohio. It has been certified for a referendum vote, but its transmission to the electorate is being postponed to allow its proponents time to conduct an educational program throughout the state. Ohioans are becoming interested in their legislative problems. Many groups such as chambers of commerce, women's clubs, citizens' leagues, and organized labor are actively sponsoring some form of unicameral legislature as the best solution. One important obstacle in the way of their success is the confusion resulting from the efforts of each group to secure support for its particular plan. A state organization has been created and a drafting committee appointed to fuse the several plans that have been proposed. There is no doubt that a reorganization of the Ohio legislature will take place if the reformers can agree to concentrate their efforts on a single plan.

CALIFORNIA

California has been dissatisfied with her legislature for some time, not with any one assembly in particular, but with the inefficiency and irresponsibility of the legislative structure as a whole. In fact, California was suspicious about the legislature when she drew up her present constitution in 1879. The time was one of turmoil, when the rampant misuse of legislative powers had aroused a widespread mistrust of legislators. As a result, the framers of California's constitution did not confine themselves to incorporating in that document only those things that are "fundamental in governmental structure or important governmental policies." They buried the organic laws under a mass of statutes which it would have been better to leave to legislative action. They included so many restrictions on the lawmakers that California's legislators have often found themselves unable to take action without an amendment to the constitution. Consequently California has developed the amending habit. More than 360 amendments have been submitted to the people and some 200 of them have been adopted. It is not unusual to find from twenty to thirty proposed amendments on the ballot at a regular election.

Some of these amendments have been attempts to reform the legislature, to make it more amenable to the public will. In 1911, when the state was swept by a wave of opposition to the control of state affairs by certain corporations, the people voted to adopt the split legislative session, hoping to secure thereby a popular review of pending legislation.[7] They were enthusiastic when the plan first went into operation in the 1913 session. During the recess many newspapers published the numbers and titles of the bills introduced, sometimes classifying them and giving a synopsis of each one. Some of the legislators conducted public discussions in their constituencies, and the citizens of Los Angeles held a convention at which they discussed the bills of particular interest. They also appointed committees to study certain measures and report their findings and opinions to the legislature when it reconvened.

That fine early enthusiasm has given way to a general dissatisfaction with the split session. The Californians have found that the recess is too short for any adequate public examination of the proposed measures but long enough for propagandist activities on the part of special interests.[8] During the 1937 session an amendment was proposed which would abolish the split session and substitute other arrange-

[7] Constitution of California, Article 4, Section 2, amended October 10, 1911. For a description of the split session as an attempt to make the legislature more responsible to the public will, see above, pages 85–86.

[8] *Franklin Hichborn's Legislative Bulletin*, January 27, 1917, p. 1. This bulletin is published at Sacramento, California.

ments for accomplishing the same purpose.[9] It would limit the period for introducing bills to forty days, after which a measure could be proposed only with the consent of three-fourths of the members. This amendment was reported favorably out of committee and passed in one house, but it was defeated on the floor of the second chamber.[10]

The problem of rural-urban representation is a serious one in California, so serious that at times during the last decade there was considerable talk about dividing the territory into two states. The residents in the north were afraid that the legislature would be controlled by the very populous Los Angeles County in the south, and the rural counties throughout the state feared the domination of the three metropolitan counties, Los Angeles, San Francisco, and Alameda.[11] It was to allay these fears that California adopted an amendment in 1926 instituting the federal plan of representation.[12] This provides for representation in the lower house according to population but in the senate according to geographic areas. No city, or county and city, is permitted to have more than one senator. The purpose of the plan, of course, is to prevent the cities from translating their population preponderance into political domination.

[9] Senate Constitutional Amendment No. 4, introduced by Senator Holohan.

[10] The initiative and referendum are used in California and stand as possible checks against unscrupulous and unwise legislation. Section 1 in Article 4 of the constitution provides: "The people reserve to themselves the power to propose laws and amendments to the Constitution, and to adopt or reject the same, at the polls independent of the Legislature, and also reserve the power, at their own option, to so adopt or reject any act, or section or part of any act, passed by the Legislature." The referendum particularly has proved very effective in California.

[11] California has fifty-eight counties with a combined population of 5,677,251. Los Angeles County is the largest of these with a population of 2,208,492; San Francisco County is second with 634,394; and Alameda County is third with 474,883 (census of 1930). Los Angeles County thus has nearly four times the population of its nearest rival in size.

[12] Constitution of California, Article 4, Section 6, amended November 26, 1926. The vote on the amendment was 437,003 in favor and 363,208 opposed.

Under this plan the three senatorial districts of Los Angeles, San Francisco, and Alameda counties contain approximately fifty-eight per cent of the state's population but are represented in the senate by only three senators, about seven and one-half per cent of the senate's voting strength. (In the assembly, where representation is based on population, Los Angeles County alone has thirty of the eighty members.) In the selection of state senators in 1934, residents of Inyo County, for example, had 120 times as much voice as a voter living in Los Angeles County. Of the 1,974,182 votes cast for state senators in the 1936 election, 1,217,265 were cast in the three metropolitan counties. Thus 61.65 per cent of the voters elected three of the senators, while 38.35 per cent elected the other thirty-seven. Such facts as these have given rise to the charge that the federal plan in operation gives disproportionate representation to rural counties, is undemocratic, and penalizes the voters living in urban communities.

Since the federal plan was proposed as a means of protecting the state from the clutch of "urban politicians" and of assuring legislation in the interests of the farmers, it was called the "dirt farmers' plan." Farm organizations in particular supported the amendment, and farm leaders stumped the state to secure its adoption.[13] But it is now generally admitted that giving rural California control of the senate has failed to benefit the farmer. Although sixteen of the senate's forty members are farmers and only seven of the assembly's eighty members belong to that class, the farmers go to the assembly when they want some piece of legislation favorable to their interests. This would seem to mean that the federal plan is no special protection for the

[13] From the filed reports listing the contributors and expenditures in the election campaign, it appears that, unknown to the farmers, the San Francisco Chamber of Commerce financed the campaign for the amendment's adoption. Its members probably preferred the control of the farmers to that of Los Angeles County.

farmers; yet some urban politicians are urging the farmers to oppose the unicameral legislature because it would eliminate that plan. In spite of their urging, the Grange, which backed the federal plan in 1926, adopted resolutions at its state convention in 1936 "endorsing the campaign for a one-house legislature" in California.

Proposing the one-house legislature as a remedy for legislative ills has been perennial in California for nearly twenty-five years. A resolution authorizing an inquiry into the advantages of that form was introduced in the constitutional convention of 1879 but was never considered on the floor. The current agitation in its favor began in 1913, when three unicameralist proposals were introduced in the legislature. Since that time nearly a score of such proposals have been considered, one or more of them in every regular legislative session except those of 1919, 1927, 1929, 1931, and 1933.[14] None of them, however, has been submitted to the vote of the people. One of the bills intro-

[14] The years and sponsors for these proposals are as follows:
1913: (a) Senate Constitutional Amendment No. 73, introduced by Senators Boynton, Carr, Cartwright, Campbell, Gates, Owen, Cohn, and Avery. (b) Assembly Constitutional Amendment No. 91 (the same as Senate Constitutional Amendment No. 73), introduced by Messrs. Bagby, Sutherland, Benedict, Weldon, W. C. Clark, Killingsworth, and Guiberson. (c) Assembly Constitutional Amendment No. 57, introduced by Mr. Farwell.
1915: (a) Senate Constitutional Amendment No. 16, introduced by Senator Campbell. (b) Assembly Constitutional Amendment No. 38 (the same as Senate Constitutional Amendment No. 16), introduced by Mr. Rigdon. (c) Assembly Constitutional Amendment No. 49, introduced by Messrs. Rominger and Dennett.
1917: (a) Senate Constitutional Amendment No. 8, introduced by Senator Brown. (b) Assembly Constitutional Amendment No. 25, introduced by Mr. Goetting.
1921: Senate Constitutional Amendment No. 18, introduced by Senators Dennett and Rominger.
1923: Senate Constitutional Amendment No. 34, introduced by Senators Dennett and Rominger.
1925: Senate Constitutional Amendment No. 15 (the same as Senate Constitutional Amendment No. 34 in 1923), introduced by Senator Dennett.
1935: (a) Senate Constitutional Amendment No. 6, introduced by Senator

duced in 1913 received affirmative votes from almost half the legislators but a two-thirds vote would have been necessary for submission.

It is possible to summarize the provisions of these various proposals, for they are similar and in some respects identical. The name most often proposed for the single chamber was the Senate, but Council of State, Legislative Assembly, and House of Representatives also appeared. Most of the earlier proposals favored a membership of forty or fifty, but the more recent proposals have increased that number, the last four being unanimous in suggesting a membership of eighty. One bill set the membership at one hundred but this number was amended to forty.[15] Most of the plans provided for a four-year term, although some recommended six years and a few two years or one. Where the length of term designated was four years or more, the amendment usually provided for rotation in the membership by election to part of the seats every two years.

Biennial sessions have been the rule, but two of the bills included annual sessions, one set a quadrennial session, and one left both the frequency and length of sessions to be determined by the legislature. Several of the plans prescribed a session of one year, to which one bill added the unusual provision "that a recess of thirty (30) days must be taken every other month beginning thirty (30) days after the first Monday after the first day of January." [16] Special sessions were provided for in all the plans, the power to call them usually being given to the governor. Most of the earlier bills set a limit of thirty days for special

McGovern. (b) Assembly Constitutional Amendment No. 69, introduced by Mr. Patterson.

1937: (a) Senate Constitutional Amendment No. 21, introduced by Senator Olson. (b) Assembly Constitutional Amendment No. 28, introduced by Mr. Heisinger. (c) Assembly Constitutional Amendment No. 33, introduced by Mr. Voigt.

[15] Senate Constitutional Amendment No. 6 (1935).

[16] Senate Constitutional Amendment No. 8 (1917).

sessions, but this restriction has disappeared in the later plans. A few of the bills applied to the new system the split session which California is using at present. That more did not do so is some indication of current opinion on that reform. One bill attempted a rather extreme safeguard against the carelessness of the last-hour rush by prohibiting action during the last month of the session on any bills except those that had been vetoed by the governor.[17]

The lieutenant governor was commonly named as the presiding officer, though with the right to vote only when necessary to break a tie. There was a marked tendency toward binding executive with legislature by giving the governor and his administrative department heads seats in the legislature, seats carrying the right to discuss but not to vote. One bill provided for executive committees which would have the power to act during recesses of the legislature.[18] Most of the proposals set the legislator's salary at $5,000 annually, but one set the sum at $3,600, one at $3,000, and one at $2,000. Two of the 1937 amendments fixed a monthly salary, $250, instead of the more common annual sum. Extra allowances for contingent expenses were generally provided for, usually by California's present method of a maximum daily sum, ranging from $250 to $500.

One of the earliest bills was marked by certain unusual features that are interesting because they imply some of the reasons motivating the proposal.[19] The bill provided

[17] *Ibid.*

[18] Senate Constitutional Amendment No. 18 (1921).

[19] Assembly Constitutional Amendment No. 57 (1913). Other amendments introduced in 1913 remind us that the proposals for a single chamber were part of a general attempt to find satisfactory reforms for the legislative structure. In that year Mr. Kingsley introduced two amendments in the assembly proposing a change in election methods. Mr. Woodly introduced Assembly Constitutional Amendment No. 93, which aimed to reduce the size of the legislature by establishing a senate of ten members and an assembly of twenty. They were to be elected from districts and were to receive a salary of $3,000 each. Contingent expenses were to be limited to $50,000 for the session. The term of office was to be eight years for senators and four years for assemblymen.

that no one could hold office in the unicameral senate if it could be proved that during the ten years preceding the election he had been employed in any capacity whatsoever by any "public utility company or corporation, any railway, or any transportation company of any sort or description, or any private or public corporation or interest or set of interests of any nature or character whatsoever." Some of the amendments added to this proposal before it was rejected are just as revealing:

The proponents or opponents of any bill or measure, under consideration by the senate, can be heard before the senate, either before the senate committee to which the measure is referred, or in the open regular session and in such manner or at such times as the senate by its rules, or by the enactment of laws on the subject may from time to time prescribe.

The proponents of any bill or measure, whether members of the senate or otherwise, may during the months of June to November of the years preceding regular sessions present their propositions to the Supreme Court, which shall clarify them, give a brief synopsis of what each contains and what it proposes to accomplish, together with their opinion thereon.

The number of bills to be introduced shall be limited to ten for each member.

Committees shall submit brief statements regarding their action on each measure considered by them.

Each member of a committee shall sign a statement that he has considered each bill for ten days, has read it through three times, and has discussed it with at least three proponents or three opponents.

Bills that are adopted shall be accompanied by statements as to their intents and purposes.

The rise of the rural-urban representation problem to its present importance can be seen very clearly in these unicameralist proposals. The earlier amendments without exception provided for the election of legislators from districts apportioned according to population, but most of those proposed since the middle 1920's have included restrictions designed to win the support of the rural areas.

Senator McGovern's proposal in 1935 authorized the legislature to divide the state into districts according to population, but it stipulated that "any county that contains population sufficient to entitle it to two or more members of the legislature shall be divided into separate and distinct legislative districts, as nearly equal in population as may be, composed of contiguous and compact territory." [20] In no event was any one county to have more than twenty-five per cent of the legislature's members.

An assembly amendment for the same year contained the provision that "four members of the legislature shall be elected from each of the said districts [twenty districts formed on the basis of population] by a plurality of the votes cast for such members by a system of voting whereby each elector may vote for not more than two candidates, the vote for one candidate to be a first choice and to count as one vote, and the vote for the other, if cast, to be a second choice and to count as a half vote." [21]

The 1937 proposals all dealt with this question of representation. One provided for election from eighty single-member districts to be determined according to population, except that no county was to be divided into more than thirty legislative districts and no county or city was to be divided unless it contained enough population within itself to form two or more districts.[22] Such an arrangement would give Los Angeles County thirty members, or $37\frac{1}{2}$ per cent of the votes in the legislature. Mr. Heisinger's assembly amendment also provided for eighty districts but stipulated that the three most populous counties were to form only thirty-three districts, the rest of the counties to form the other forty-seven. As a concession to the urban interests, the amendment provided that no county in the latter group was to have more than three districts.

[20] Senate Constitutional Amendment No. 6 (1935).
[21] Assembly Constitutional Amendment No. 69 (1935).
[22] Senate Constitutional Amendment No. 21 (1937).

THE UNICAMERAL LEGISLATURE

It is clear that any proposal for a one-house legislature which is to win enough support for adoption in California must solve this representation problem in a way that will satisfy both rural and urban interests. This solution may be found in the suggested two-fifths–three-fifths plan of apportionment, according to which two-fifths of the legislators would be elected from the three metropolitan counties and the other three-fifths from the remaining fifty-five counties. A modification of this apportionment would allow the three counties to select one half of the legislators and the fifty-five counties the other half.

There is no reason to believe that this matter cannot be handled as adequately in a single house as in the present two houses. At any rate, it is likely that a unicameralist amendment will be submitted to the voters in the near future. Either that, or a convention will be called to overhaul the entire constitution. Changes in California's legislative structure are likely to be made soon, but that these will bring a unicameral legislature is less certain.

7

NEBRASKA ADOPTS A SINGLE-CHAMBER LEGISLATURE

Nebraska's bicameral legislature. — Most of the evils charged to the bicameral system were present to some degree in Nebraska's two-house legislature. Her two chambers almost duplicated each other in the qualifications, constituencies, terms, salaries, duties, and procedures of their respective memberships. They passed approximately three hundred and fifty of the one thousand bills introduced at an average session, and they rushed many of them through during the closing days of the session. They both dodged responsibility by shifting it onto the other house or onto a conference committee.

In fact their record furnishes a good example of the power of the conference committee. A study of the legislatures from 1921 to 1933 has shown that 10.95 per cent of all the measures passed by both houses during the regular sessions had passed through the conference committee and "27.24 per cent of all bills amended by the second house and finally passed by the legislature were sent to conference."[1] Many of these were very important measures, such as the regular biennial appropriation bills, which always had to be referred to conference.

It was the common practice to appoint most of these joint

[1] Franklin L. Burdette, "Conference Committees in the Nebraska Legislature," *American Political Science Review,* 30:1114 (December, 1936).

committees near the end of the session. Of all the bills sent to conference during the twelve years from 1921 to 1933, 69.14 per cent were sent during the last twenty days of the session and 49.71 per cent during the last ten days. Membership on the conference groups was well distributed in the course of the session. An average of 87 per cent of the senators and 48.71 per cent of the representatives served on the committees. Even the original sponsors of the bill were sometimes included on the revising committee. An account of what the committees did to the bills they considered is contained in the following passage:

In the case of well over half of the conference bills which ultimately passed, the committee made material changes in subject-matter, either in the original text or in the amendments. Among the five general types of conference reports, the percentage of bills which belonged to each classification were: (1) to make a material change, 63.35 per cent; (2) to adopt the amendments of the second house, 13.04 per cent; (3) to recommend that the second house recede from its amendments, 11.18 per cent; (4) to propose that part of the amendments be adopted and that the second chamber recede from part, 11.18 per cent; and (5) to suggest only technical or clarifying alterations, 1.24 per cent. Exactly 92 per cent of all conference bills were passed by the legislature. In the case of 74.29 per cent of all bills sent to conference, only one meeting of the conferees was required. For the remainder, from two to four meetings were necessary.[2]

But there was nothing much out of the ordinary in the record of the Nebraska legislature. As Professor Lancaster says, there was about the usual "bickering, back scratching, log-rolling, horse play and general blowing off of steam to which democratic assemblies are addicted."[3] The following paragraph summarizes a trained observer's conclusions about the Nebraska legislators and legislative methods in 1924:

[2] *Ibid.*
[3] Lane W. Lancaster, "Nebraska Prunes Her Legislature," *Current History*, 41:434–36 (January, 1935).

In conclusion it may be said that the legislators are perhaps on the whole seriously minded toward their obligations and fairly representative members of their communities though not possessed of any special qualifications for their tasks and not very open-minded, inclined rather to retain their prejudices and traditional views in the face of new ideas. The first step in legislation, — the determination of the fields within which action shall be taken, — is pretty poorly performed. Parties and governors and legislative leaders are generally slow to present a program of legislation, or else present it in such a way that little state-wide expression of opinion is secured. Provision is made for the technical preparation of legislation, but members do not take advantage sufficiently of the opportunities of assistance in this work, and are lacking in aggressiveness in running down independent information as a basis of their decisions. The committee system is fairly adequate, but here, as else-where, committees may be informed when the houses are not. The lobby is probably the most important source of information or misinformation. The machinery proper for the enactment of laws is quite satisfactory. There is a large opportunity for discussion, little effort at sharp practices, and in general conditions exist which support the impression that the product of the legislative mill is not widely different from what it would be if the citizen body could be substituted for the official lawmakers. Probably, however, the product of a representative assembly ought to be better than that of a primary assembly.[4]

The movement for unicameralism. — Although this description reveals no particular aggravation of legislative difficulties, the movement for unicameralism as a means of reform began early in Nebraska and has reached fruition. In 1913, the year that Governor Hodges proposed the novel single-house assembly to the people of Kansas, a joint committee of Nebraska legislators was appointed to study ways and means for improving legislative procedure. When the committee made its report to the 1915 session, it recom-

---

[4] Ralph S. Boots, "Our Legislative Mills: Nebraska, How the Legislature Behaves Itself in a State in Which the Individual Members Pride Themselves on Independence of a Tight Political Machine," *National Municipal Review*, 13:111 (February, 1924).

mended that an amendment establishing a single chamber be submitted to the people. The session did not act upon this recommendation. The proposition reappeared in the 1917 session but failed to pass. When it came up in the constitutional convention of 1919–20, it received a tie vote, which was broken by the president's voting in the negative.[5] An initiative petition circulated in 1923 failed to get enough signatures, and the proposals introduced in the legislative sessions of 1923, 1925, and 1933 received little serious consideration. Nonetheless, all this agitation was not fruitless for it educated the public to the idea of a single house and helped to make it ready for the campaign in 1934.

Senator George W. Norris had long been the moving spirit in the agitation for a unicameral legislature, and he gave all his efforts to the cause in the spring and summer of 1934. He put his ideas before the people in writing and in public addresses. He maintained that the experience of a hundred years had demonstrated that bicameral legislatures in state governments give very unsatisfactory results. He admitted the need for the conference committee under the bicameral system, but asserted that such committees were responsible for many legislative evils, that "jokers get into legislation" in the conference committee room. He insisted that experience had shown that "large membership is detrimental to real representation," and he advocated a small assembly in order to make it impossible for the individual legislator to conceal his record or to shift responsibility to the other house. He pointed out that a smaller body would save money for the taxpayer even while it permitted the increase in salaries necessary to attract capable men.

Senator Norris' idea was to establish a group of legislative experts who would be in almost continuous session,

[5] Proceedings of the Nebraska Constitutional Convention, 1919–20, p. 2798.

would give their undivided attention to the affairs of the state, and would perform duties analogous to those of the board of directors in a corporation. To this end he also suggested a four-year term, with the recall as a safeguard. Hoping for legislators who would work for the welfare of the state, he urged that party issues be taken out of the legislative chamber by use of the nonpartisan ballot. He called attention to the fact that such problems of the federal government as the tariff, immigration, military preparedness, and federal subsidies, which may possibly require party alignments, are not present in the states.

The 1934 amendment. — Under Senator Norris' leadership, a citizens' committee drafted an amendment to be submitted to the people by means of the initiative. The amendment provided for a chamber of from thirty to fifty members, leaving it to the legislature to determine the exact number within the specified range. To ensure keeping the number as low as possible, the amendment stipulated that the "aggregate salaries of all members shall be $37,500 per annum." Since the sum was to be divided equally among all the legislators, the larger the legislature the lower each man's salary. If the minimum of members were chosen, this scheme would provide a salary lower than the $2,400 advocated by Senator Norris, but more than the $800 which legislators were then receiving. In addition each member was to receive the amount of his expenses, traveling by the "most usual route once to and returning from each regular or special session of the legislature."

Since the plan, if adopted, was to go into operation in the 1937 session, the legislature of 1935 was to divide the state into single-member districts on the basis of population, excluding aliens. Reapportionment was to take place whenever it was needed to prevent inequalities in representation, but not oftener than once every ten years.

Both two-year terms and biennial sessions were prescribed in the amendment, but a provision was added to permit changing the frequency of session either by constitutional amendment or by law. The lieutenant governor was to be the presiding officer of the new assembly, which was to elect all other officers, including a speaker to preside in the absence of the lieutenant governor. Hoping to impose a check on careless lawmaking, the drafting committee included a requirement that the final vote should not be cast on any bill until five legislative days after its introduction and not until it had been on file "for final reading and passage for at least one legislative day."

An important provision required the election of members on a nonpartisan ballot. This plan was not new in Nebraska. It had previously been adopted for the election of judges, school officials, regents of the state university, and many municipal officers, partly as a way of making these officials independent of the governor, who had at times secured an undesirable extent of control over them.

These were the principal provisions of the amendment placed before the people in 1934. The time was opportune. A great deal of discussion had resulted from the 1933 legislative session, when members had boasted that they were "going to the capitol to pass a few laws, to talk a little, and to return home in time for the spring plowing." Their boast was idle in at least one respect, for the 1933 session was one of the longest on record in Nebraska and passed nearly two hundred bills. There was much wrangling over such questions as taxation, appropriations, liquor, and legislative apportionments, but there were few real accomplishments. The legislature was composed largely of inexperienced members, who had been swept into office in the landslide of 1932, and it lacked effective leadership because of the governor's illness. All of this helped to make the legislature unpopular and to deepen the unfavorable impression of legislative efficiency in the minds of Nebraska's citizens — just at the time when New Deal policies and measures were bringing the idea of experimentation into the air.[6]

In 1934 an initiative petition had to secure 57,000 signatures, ten per cent of the total vote cast in the previous election. By June 5, a month before the specified time limit, 75,000 persons had signed. The people were willing to vote on the experiment at least.[7] The amendment was debated with vigor before the election in November. Those who opposed it offered the usual arguments. They declared that the farmers would not be properly represented in so small a body, that a single chamber would give scheming politicians and unscrupulous pressure groups more opportunity to gain their ends, and that measures would receive less thorough discussion. They insisted that a small group would be more extravagant and that only the rich would be able to campaign in the large electoral districts which would result from having so few representatives. They said that limiting the representation was undemocratic, and they emphasized the wisdom of the founding fathers in setting up the checks and balances of the bicameral system. Many were sincere in these arguments; others used them chiefly because they disliked the plan's principal sponsor for his consistently ultraliberal policies. The newspapers of the state were largely in sympathy with this opposition. They were either noncommittal or openly opposed to the proposed change.[8]

But the promoters of the amendment were confident. They pointed out the success of unicameralism in the Canadian provinces and dwelt upon the disgrace of a gov-

[6] Lane W. Lancaster, "Nebraska Considers a One-House Legislature," *National Municipal Review*, 23:373–76 (July, 1934).

[7] Lester B. Orfield, "The Unicameral Legislature in Nebraska," *Michigan Law Review*, 34:26–36 (November, 1935).

[8] John P. Senning, "Nebraska Provides for a One-House Legislature," *American Political Science Review*, 29:69 (February, 1935). See also, by the same author, *The One-House Legislature* (New York, 1937).

ernment structure still in the "ox-cart age" in this day of automobile and airplane. They won the day. The amendment was adopted by a majority of more than 90,000. The vote was 286,086 for the plan and 193,152 against it. Only nine of the state's ninety-three counties failed to approve it.

Since the amendment was to go into effect in 1937, it was the task of the 1935 legislature to determine the exact number of members and to establish the legislative districts. The committee charged with the task wisely let the number of districts that would provide the fairest distribution between urban east and agricultural west determine the number of legislators. This was found to be forty-three, which meant one representative for each 32,471 persons, excluding aliens. Douglas County, including the city of Omaha, was assigned seven representatives and Lancaster County, including Lincoln, three representatives. Each of the legislators was to receive $1,744.18 for the two-year term, plus the cost of one round trip from his home to the capital during each session.

Results of the 1936 elections. — The elections in 1936 brought more aspirants for membership in the new unicameral legislature than had been usual under the bicameral system. The total number entered in the primary elections was 283 for the 43 districts, averaging 6.58 persons per district, but ranging from three aspirants in the first district to twenty in the tenth. Among the entrants, those who had been legislators before and especially those who had served in the last session were given preference by the voters. Of the forty-three elected, thirty-two had had previous experience in one or both houses of the bicameral legislature. The results of the election gave promise of a truly nonpartisan assembly. Of the 133 members elected to the legislature in 1934, 90 were Democrats and only 21 Republicans. But in 1936 there were 45 Democrat and 41 Republican candidates in the final election, and the successful group included 22 Democrats and 21 Republicans. In about half of the districts the two candidates were members of the same party.

The range of ages among the new legislators was from twenty-six to seventy-two years, with the average at approximately forty-eight. There were no women members, although there had been from one to three women in every session since 1923 and although there were seven women entered in the primary and two in the final election. Eighteen farmers and ten lawyers were elected; other occupations represented ranged from the "general mercantile business to athletic coaching and veterinary surgery." Twenty-seven of the members had attended college, and about twenty of them held one or more degrees. The majority were Nebraska-born, but some were natives of other states and a few were natives of other countries, including one born in Germany, one in New Brunswick, and one in Sweden.

Opinion is divided as to whether Nebraska's first one-house legislature secured the services of more capable men, as its advocates had claimed it would. The thirty-two members who had served before could hardly claim to be better than they had been under the bicameral system; but it is Professor Aylsworth's opinion that the members of the first unicameral assembly were "rather better equipped in native ability, educational training, and legislative experience for the task facing them than those of any legislature in many years." [9] Others maintain that although the body is smaller and the number of misfits therefore lower, few of the members are superior to their predecessors, and that they have the same propensities for dodging roll calls and escaping responsibility as before.

The work of the first unicameral session. — The unicameral legislature opened its initial session on January 5,

[9] L. E. Aylsworth, "Nebraska's Nonpartisan Unicameral Legislature," *National Municipal Review,* 26:77–81 (February, 1937).

1937. Nearly a century had passed since the last unicameral state legislature met, and the eyes, not only of Nebraskans, but of citizens throughout the nation, were turned to watch this experiment in government. The galleries were crowded. Senator Norris was present and was invited to address the assembly. He spoke briefly, stressing the more-than-local importance of the assemblage and of the record it would write. He said in part:

Everything that special interests can do to embarrass you, and to misinterpret your action, will be attempted. On the other hand, every lover of his fellow men, every person who wants to place our state on a higher standard of efficiency, every person who is anxious to bring about improvement in our state affairs, every patriot who wants to place our government on a higher level for good, every lover of human liberty and equal justice, and every believer in the business administration of state affairs as distinguished from political machine control, is hoping, praying and believing that your official work will be crowned with unlimited success to the satisfaction and approval of believers in good government everywhere.

Almost the entire first month of the session was occupied with the organization of committees and the adoption of rules of procedure. These were highly important tasks but not simple ones. On the recommendation of the committee on committees, the legislature established fifteen standing committees, organized on the basis of the major fields of legislation and ranging in membership from five to eleven, as follows: agriculture, eleven members; appropriations, eleven; banking and insurance, seven; claims and deficiencies, five; commerce and communications, five; drainage, irrigation, and water power, seven; education, nine; enrollment and review, five; government, nine; judiciary, nine; labor and public welfare, nine; legislation and administration, five; public health and miscellaneous, seven; public highways and bridges, seven; and revenue, nine. Added to the committee on committees and the committee on rules these make a total of seventeen, in contrast to the sixty-eight in the preceding legislature (thirty-two in the senate and thirty-six in the house).

By adopting a rule that standing committees should elect their own presiding officers, the legislature eliminated what had always been considered one of the choicest morsels for the dominant party, the right of naming committee chairmen. This had previously been a function of the chairman of the committee on committees, but the proposal to keep it as such was defeated on the floor. In order to fill the 124 committee assignments it was necessary to appoint every legislator to three committees and some to four. The legislature voted to reserve the afternoons for committee sessions, and each member had a session to attend every afternoon, but only one, for a schedule of meetings was arranged to prevent the overlapping of appointments that had characterized bicameral sessions.

An innovation in procedure that aroused widespread enthusiasm was the institution of a public hearing on every bill while it was in committee. The time and place for the hearing were announced in the newspapers, the legislative journal, and on the bulletin boards at least five days before the date set. This was one step in abolishing the relic of secret sessions. Another was requiring the filing of a complete report of committee action on every bill, stating the reasons for any changes proposed and the opinions of the various committee members. These reports are not published except by request, but they are kept available for inspection in the office of the secretary of state. Copies of committee roll-call votes are printed in the official legislative journal.

The only objection from the floor to the report of the committee on rules was raised on the question of the committee of the whole. The report was in favor of continuing that device, but the committee had split on the question and its chairman carried the discussion to the assembly. Some contended that the extra check provided by the action of the committee of the whole was especially necessary in a legislature of one house. They felt, too, that sessions of that committee provided a round table discussion which gave to "every member his day in court." Others argued that such a committee was not needed in a nonpartisan chamber. They pointed out that retaining it would mean added expense and undue delay in the legislature's action. They estimated that, barring the suspension of the rules, it would require a minimum of fourteen days for a bill to pass from introduction to adoption. Action by the committee of the whole would extend that time and would also provide a way of dodging responsibility. Wishing to prevent careless haste and ensure time for deliberation, the majority were persuaded to retain the committee. They provided, however, for a roll-call vote in its sessions whenever called for by any member. Toward the end of the session, it was decided to try getting along without the committee of the whole, and its use was suspended for the remainder of the session without a dissenting vote.

After a measure has been reported favorably out of committee and has passed its first consideration by the house, it is referred to the committee on enrollment and review for a thorough examination as to phraseology and constitutionality. If it passes this scrutiny, it is placed in a special file for a second consideration before it appears on the calendar for its third and final reading. From three to five days must elapse between these various stages. This procedure is a valuable contribution to lawmaking, but it can be used only in a unicameral body, for neither house has full control of a bill under the bicameral organization. Moreover, where there is no shuttling of measures back and forth between houses such a routine procedure permits the public to follow the progress of a bill with ease.

Under the bicameral system in Nebraska, the period for introducing the bills was limited to the first twenty days of the session. Interpreting this restriction as a "box in which the governor had the legislature," the framers of the unicameralist amendment discarded it. The legislature restored it but extended the period to thirty days. The general appropriation bill may be introduced up to and including the fortieth day, but other bills may be proposed after the thirtieth day only at the request of the governor or by a two-thirds vote of the legislature. There is no prescribed length for the session; it continues "at the pleasure of the legislature."

At the recommendation of the judiciary committee, the legislature employed an expert bill-drafter and two lawyers to advise the members on the constitutionality of pending legislation. The strong sentiment for establishing a legislative council which appeared early in the session bore fruit in a law creating a council of ten members, plus the speaker of the senate as a member ex officio. The council is to meet at least twice a year, is to gather information for the legislature, and is to prepare "a legislative program in the form of bills or otherwise as in its opinion the welfare of the state may require." One other of the session's measures pertained to the legislature; it permitted the calling of an annual or special session upon the request of twenty-nine legislators with or without the concurrence of the governor.

Perhaps the most important action during the session was the passage of a measure for submitting a short ballot proposal to the people. This would mean the election of the governor, lieutenant governor, superintendent of public instruction, and state auditor for four-year terms and the appointment of the secretary of state, treasurer, and attorney general by the legislature. Such a proposal has been introduced many times before, but it always failed to pass in the bicameral legislature. The unicameral session also acted upon such matters as unemployment insurance, social security, liquor control, and a mortgage moratorium.

When the thirty-day limit was reached, 551 bills had been introduced, 211 of them on the thirtieth day. This was more than the number introduced on the last day in either of the houses in 1935, but less than the total of 283 for both houses. The number of bills introduced during the session averaged 12.8 per member, which was higher than in 1935 but just about one-half the total number for the preceding session. Here is an interesting statistical comparison of the two sessions:[10]

	Bicameral, 1935	Unicameral, 1937
Cost of session	$202,500	$150,000
Bills introduced	1,056	581
Bills passed	192	210
Bills vetoed	6	18
Length of session	110 days	98 days

Evaluation of the first unicameral session. — Opinions of the work of this first unicameral session vary widely. Some to whom the unicameral legislature was oversold are disappointed because it has not proved a quick panacea. In the enthusiasm of the campaign, they were led to forget that the new "streamlined" legislature would still be composed of ordinary persons.[11] There are others who find in the session of 1937 justification for their most extravagant claims; many who find plenty to criticize; a few who find support for their worst fears. As one writer has facetiously described the state of opinion,

The before and after effects of taking unicameral are difficult to determine. Some have rushed in to sign testimonials saying one bottle made them jump up and dance jigs after they had

[10] Kenneth Keller in "Nebraska's Unicameral Adjourns," *State Government*, 10:134 (July, 1937). This article is a collection of opinions on the first session of Nebraska's unicameral legislature, one of which is by Mr. Keller, a newspaper reporter who covered the session for the *Lincoln Star*.
[11] *Ibid.*

been bedfast for years and the best doctors had given up hope. Others say it is the alcohol or power of suggestion and that there is little medicinal value apparent and may not be for years to come, and maybe they were going to get well anyway and that their time had not really come, or that they are just kidding themselves, or that the germ theory still holds true, or that the law of Mendel will get them and legislators will revert to type if you give them time.[12]

What support is there for these varying opinions? How well did the first unicameral body realize the promise offered by a nonpartisan legislature owing allegiance to no politician and free to write a splendid record in the interests of the people and of good government? Observers are quite well agreed that the members made a sincere effort to be nonpartisan and succeeded to a heartening degree. There was no noticeable partisanship in determining the committee memberships or their chairmen. Seven members of the committee on committees were Democrats and five were Republicans. Eleven of the committee chairmen (elected by the committees, not appointed) were Democrats and six Republicans. The chairman of the highly important appropriations committee, for instance, was Republican Frank J. Brady, although if classified on party lines, the senate had a Democratic majority. Similarly, in the election of the speaker the two rival candidates were Charles J. Warner, who had previously served as Republican floor leader in both the senate and the house, and W. F. Haycock, who had been the Democratic floor leader in the 1935 session. But the "Democratic" assembly elected the Republican Warner. Party alignments on the legislation considered were evident in only a few instances, and their appearing at all has been attributed to the presence of a few old party "warhorses" among the members.[13] In summary, this first session justifies the belief that party allegiance will

[12] *Nebraska State Journal*, (March 8, 1937).
[13] Keller in "Nebraska's Unicameral Adjourns," p. 133.

cease entirely to be a dividing factor in Nebraska's legislature when a few more sessions have developed a group of statesmen accustomed to nonpartisanship.

Though this nonpolitical character was considered the best feature of the experiment by one senator, it was the factor which the governor chose to blame for most of the difficulties that appeared.[14] Nonetheless, the session was noteworthy for the harmony that prevailed between the executive and the legislature. It furnished little support for the contention that there must be friction between a nonpartisan single-chamber legislature and a governor elected on a party platform and with party commitments. Very early in the session, the governor announced that he did not intend to take any part in legislative affairs or to exert any influence in the selection of officers or the formulation of policies. He offered his cooperation in making the session successful and pledged his department to respect the nonpartisan character of the legislature.

Many observers point out that the unicameral house adopted pieces of progressive legislation which had been defeated repeatedly in the two-house legislature. Others found it much less radical than they had hoped. Most were disappointed when it refused to ratify the child labor amendment. Making the legislature unicameral did not eliminate committees. Much of the work must still be done in these smaller groups, so that members must vote more or less blindly on a good many measures. But no one can deny that the organization and procedure adopted for the committees of the Nebraska single house are a vast improvement over most. Could they have been achieved without the convenient occasion of instituting the single chamber?

Another marked improvement was the bringing of all procedure into the open. As one writer has observed,

[14] See the opinions of Senator O. Edwin Schultz and Governor Robert L. Cochran in "Nebraska's Unicameral Adjourns."

"Whatever else can be said, the unicameral legislature moved the session from hotel rooms to the capitol." [15] This feature, with the individual accountability which it ensures, won special approval from Senator Norris, who wrote:

There has not been an instance during this session where this legislature could have indulged in the old familiar dodge of "passing the buck" from one house to the other, and from both houses to the conference committee. Every member had an increased responsibility and realized as never before the responsibility of his position. The possibilities are that the next unicameral legislature will be superior to the present one for the reason that the people will have had an opportunity to vote out of office any member who, in their judgment, has proved false to his trust.[16]

This leads us to ask how the lobby fared in the new assembly. Here, perhaps, occurs the widest divergence of opinion. "Some are sure that the lobbyists will become the *de facto* legislators; others see no pronounced change from the bicameral years, and still others, the avowed proponents of unicameralism, aver that the lobbying situation has been substantially improved by the new system." [17] The first group finds plenty of reason for its fears. The sessions of the new assembly are held in the chamber formerly used by the lower house, and the seating of the forty-three members left some sixty empty seats in the back of the room. These were assigned to the lobbyists.

And so you have the spectacle of elected representatives of the people sitting sedately at the front of the hall, legislating for the public welfare under the constant scrutiny of three-score other official representatives — the representatives of special interests. It is truly instructive to the uninitiated to witness such stark realism in a legislative assembly. . . . Only a fabric cord

[15] Keller in "Nebraska's Unicameral Adjourns," p. 134.
[16] "Nebraska's Unicameral Adjourns," p. 132.
[17] Cortez A. M. Ewing, "Lobbying in Nebraska's Legislature," *Public Opinion Quarterly*, 1:102 (July, 1937).

divides the legislators from the lobbyists. Such demarcation can be no more than a legal fiction.[18]

No wonder that one lobbyist called the unicameral legislature "a lobbyist's paradise," and added, "Why, there are four or five official lobbyists for every legislative member! There is more pressure here than I have ever witnessed in a Nebraska legislative session!" [19]

Everyone admits that the lobby had plenty of power but there is a counterbalancing factor in the fact that its power and pressure were conspicuous, not hidden. One factor of weight in determining a lobbyist's influence is the elective nature of the legislator's position. Since roll-call votes are easy to secure in all executive sessions, since all committee action is reported and made public, and since newspapermen are permitted to attend and report committee sessions, a legislator may jeopardize his political position by succumbing to the proposals of the lobby. The threat of retirement from office will certainly give the legislator more courage to withstand the lobbyist's pressure. One of the Nebraska senators outlined this situation thus:

It is important to remember that while the lobbyist had fewer lawmakers to deal with, which may have made it easier for him, he could not avoid placing his friends on the spot. His allies on the floor were plainly known in the unicameral, and not concealed as in the two-house sessions. Thus the lobbyist was brought out in the open and occupied the same spot as his lawmaking allies.[20]

To which we may add the statement of one of the lobbyists, "It's different working with the unicameral, but it isn't easier." [21] After studying the situation and these opinions pro and con, Cortez Ewing, director of the School of Citi-

[18] *Ibid.*

[19] *Ibid.*, p. 103.

[20] Senator Emil M. Von Seggern in "Nebraska's Unicameral Adjourns," p. 133.

[21] Quoted by Keller in "Nebraska's Unicameral Adjourns," p. 134.

zenship and Public Affairs at the University of Oklahoma, concluded that the unicameral system has at least not increased the effectiveness of the lobby in the Nebraska legislature.[22]

Many observers were impressed by the informality which characterized the single chamber's deliberations, without causing any significant loss of dignity. The sessions were like round table conferences, the members speaking without oratory and without the formality of recognition by the speaker. Many legislators who might have hesitated to address the group formally participated freely in these discussions. Most of the members seemed very much in earnest, apparently aware that their action was final, that it would not be reviewed in a second chamber.[23] The number of vetoes imposed by the governor, however, may indicate that the unicameral assembly expected — or at least allowed — the executive to act as the "other house." This gives the governor not only more responsibility but also more power.

Many have criticized this legislature for introducing too many bills, enacting too many laws, and remaining in session too long.[24] Friends of the system reply that the length of the session was partly due to the difficulty of formulating new rules and that the surplus of legislation is mainly the fault of the constituents, not of the legislators. The people still look upon the lawmakers as agents of particular localities rather than of the state as a whole. They insist that their representative introduce bills dealing with local or personal matters which do not require legislative action. Local governments are likely to refer their difficult prob-

[22] "Lobbying in the Nebraska Legislature," p. 103.

[23] Elizabeth Senning, *Nebraska's One-House Legislature* (University of Nebraska Cooperative Extension Work in Agriculture and Home Economics, Extension Circular 5542, 1937), p. 7. This is a mimeographed bulletin.

[24] *Ibid.,* p. 8.

lems to the state legislature for solving, and the legislature is inclined to act upon matters which should be left to the administrative departments. Nebraska has modernized its legislative machinery; it needs also to modernize its political thinking.[25]

It is, of course, unfair to pass judgment on the unicameral system on the basis of one session of one legislature. Time and more experience will bring adjustments and perhaps modifications. But it is interesting to note that one of the senators in the Nebraska chamber is certain that "if the future shows necessity for change, it will not be reversion to the two-house system, but improvement of the one-house plan." [26]

[25] *Ibid.,* pp. 8–9.
[26] Senator Emil M. Von Seggern in "Nebraska's Unicameral Adjourns," p. 133. For a description and evaluation of this first unicameral session, see Lane W. Lancaster, "Nebraska's New Legislature," *Minnesota Law Review,* 22: 60–77 (December, 1937).

8

WHAT OF THE FUTURE?

WE TURN now from recounting details to a consideration of the general tendencies evident in the facts we have cited. No one denies the need for reform in our legislative structure, and the proposals for a unicameral legislature are only one phase of a broad movement to make our legislative organization more efficient and to improve the quality of its product. Although not all the advocates of reform will concede that the only logical and adequate solution for the present ills is to discard the bicameral form and establish the one-house legislature in its stead, the support for that idea is growing, as the number of recent amendments embodying it seems to indicate. A study of the forty measures introduced during the 1937 sessions shows that the general form likely to be taken by unicameral legislatures has already crystallized. Certain definite trends in organization and procedure are apparent in the accompanying tabular analysis on pages 152–55.

Legislature size. — Thirty-two of the bills tabulated stipulate the size of the chamber, which ranges from 15 members in Wyoming to 200 members in Pennsylvania and 240 members in Massachusetts. Some bills merely specify a minimum and maximum number, leaving the exact number to be determined by the legislature. Of those which prescribe the number, two specify a membership of 15 to 30; five stipulate 30 to 50; two, 46 to 60; two, 60; and three,

80. Only seven recommend a membership exceeding one hundred. Sixteen prescribe a range of 15 to 52, and the average membership for all the proposals is between 62 and 63 members. The Nebraska amendment permitted a membership of from 30 to 50, and the legislature set the number at 43.

The advantages sought in the adoption of a unicameral legislature would be more readily achieved by a comparatively small body. Of course, the size of the state and the number of interests to be represented should help to determine the number of legislators, but for a small state with few distinct groups to be represented, a legislative body of from forty to sixty members will be the most effective. A large industrial state should probably have from eighty to one hundred members in order to ensure adequate representation to the various interests in the state. These numbers may be increased slightly if the people demand it, but even in our largest and most complex states the legislature should not much exceed one hundred if the maximum benefits are to be secured from a unicameral legislature.

Method of electing the legislators. — The question of how the members of the legislature are to be chosen is not a simple one. Of the thirty-six amendments that prescribe the method of election, twenty-three follow the Nebraska practice of election from single-member districts formed on the basis of population. Seven proposals would modify the single-member–district plan by county restrictions, two provide for elections by counties, one by congressional districts, one by double-member districts, one by quadruple-member districts, and one by districts according to party strength with a single transferable vote. Some of the plans make use of a district large enough to permit the election of four or five members, in that way allowing to minority groups a representation denied them in the single-member districts under the plurality plan of voting. Cumulative voting is possible in districts from which at least three or four members may be elected.[1] Something approximating this arrangement is a feature of the Massachusetts plan.

In states which, like Nebraska, are largely agricultural, with few large cities and few diversified interests to be represented, single-member districts equally apportioned according to population are satisfactory. But in states like California, New York, or Ohio, where the rural-urban issue in representation has become a real problem, there is a strong demand for some representation on the basis of geographical areas. Rural areas have won a dominant position in many legislatures, which they do not wish to relinquish, contending that the cities in their rapid growth have developed views that do not recognize the needs of the rural sections. The unicameral legislature offers no barrier to a fair solution of this problem. Some of the unicameralist proposals that have been made in California and Ohio show that an adjustment of representation can be made almost as easily in a single chamber as in the bicameral assembly.[2]

Term of office. — Of the thirty-six proposed amendments which prescribe a definite tenure, twelve set a four-year term; twenty retain the two-year term which is general under the bicameral system; one calls for annual elections; and three set different terms for county and district members. When the amendment was being considered in Nebraska there were a number of people, including Senator Norris, who favored a four- or six-year term, but the more common biennial election was finally approved.

Logic would favor the longer term, since that would give the incumbents time to become better acquainted with their duties and to demonstrate their abilities to their con-

[1] See above, page 79, for an explanation of cumulative voting.
[2] For the rural-urban problems and proposed solutions in Ohio and California, see above, pages 116–17, 121–23, 126–28.

CONSTITUTIONAL AMENDMENTS PROPOSED IN 1937 FOR THE CREATION OF UNICAMERAL LEGISLATURES[a]

Proposed Amendments	Salary	Term (in years)	Non-partisan	Size	Elective Districts	Presiding Officer	Initiative	Referendum	Maximum Length of Session	Frequency of Session
ARKANSAS H.J.R. No. 1 (Campbell)	$1500 a year	2; 4 if reelected	Yes	50	Single-member districts by population; no more than 2 counties added	Lt. Gov.			Indefinite; maximum expense $50,000	Biennial
CALIFORNIA S.C.A. No. 21 (Olson)	$250 a month	2		80	Single-member districts by population; maximum of 30 districts to any county	Lt. Gov.	Yes	Yes	Indefinite	Annual
CALIFORNIA A.C.A. No. 28 (Heisinger)	$250 a month	4[b]		80	Single-member districts by population; 33 districts in the 3 metropolitan counties	Lt. Gov.	Yes	Yes	30 days, then recess 30 days (bifurcation plan)	Biennial
CALIFORNIA A.C.A. No. 33 (Voigt)	$3600 a year	1		80	Single-member districts by population	Elected by legislature	Yes	Yes	30 days, then recess 30 days	Annual
GEORGIA H.B. No. 280 (Sanders)	$15 a day maximum	4		52	Single-member districts; all three-county, except 7 four-county; 1 one-county; and 1 two-county	Lt. Gov.			60 days	Biennial
IDAHO H.J.R. No. 8 (Coker)	$5 a day minimum; $2500–$3000 a year for committeemen	2	Permissible	27–59	Single-member districts by population	Lt. Gov.	Yes	Yes	1st session, 10–12 days; 2d session not specified	Biennial
IOWA H.J.R. No. 4 (Foster)		2	Yes	Minimum 99	Apparently by counties. At least 1 from each county	Lt. Gov.			Indefinite	Biennial
KANSAS S.C.R. No. 5 (Benson)	$8 a day up to $400; special session up to $140	2	Yes	30–50	Single-member districts by population	Lt. Gov.				Biennial
KANSAS H.C.R. No. 9 (Ryan)	$8 a day up to $400; special session up to $140	2	Yes	30–50	Single-member districts by population	Lt. Gov.				Biennial
MASSACHUSETTS H. No. 1081 (Morrill)				240	By districts or at large; representation in proportion to party strength					
MINNESOTA S.B. No. 197 (Johnson) H.F. No. 214 (Pederson)	To be determined	2		To be prescribed by law	Single-member districts by population	Lt. Gov.				Biennial

State / Bill	Compensation	Term		Size	Apportionment	Presiding officer		Session	
MINNESOTA S.B. No. 452 (McLeod)	$2500–$5000 a year	4[b]		30–50	Single-member districts by population	Lt. Gov.	Yes	90 days	Biennial
MINNESOTA H.F. No. 1091 (Nielsen and Nordin)	To be determined	2		131–45	Single-member districts by population	Lt. Gov.	Yes		Biennial
MONTANA H.B. No. 73 (Measure)	$1000 a biennium	4[b]	Yes	56–80 (78 1st session)	Each county 1 member, with specified exceptions		Yes		Biennial
NEVADA A.J.R. No. 20 (Tallman)	Indefinite	4		17	One member from each county	Elected by legislature	Yes	60 days; special session 20 days	Biennial
NEVADA A.J.R. No. 22 (Bugbee and 4 others)	Indefinite	2	Yes		Single-member districts by population	Lt. Gov.	Yes	1st session 90 days; following sessions 60; special session 20 days	Annual
NEW JERSEY S.C.R. No. 1 (Bowers)	$120,000 divided equally	2	Yes	Maximum 60	Single-member districts by population	Elected by legislature	Yes		Biennial
NEW MEXICO S.J.R. No. 5 (Kennedy, Harrelson, and Eager)		4		31–40	Single-member districts by population	Lt. Gov.	Yes		
NORTH DAKOTA H.C.R. "R" (Kapaun, Gilberg, and Holm)	$600 a session	4[b]	Yes	30–50	Single-member districts by population	Lt. Gov.	Yes	1st session 30 days; 2d session 60 days	Biennial
OHIO H.J.R. No. 10 (Thorne)		2		To be determined			Yes		
OHIO H.J.R. No. 11 (Kasch)	$3600 a year to county, $6000 a year to district members	County, 2; District, 4			As at present for congressional districts	Lt. Gov.	Yes		
OHIO H.J.R. No. 16 (Harter)		2		80	1 member for each 1/80 of the state's population in each county	Lt. Gov.	Yes		Recess only 3 months at a time
OHIO H.J.R. No. 26 (Hudlett)	To be determined	Sen. 4; Rep. 2			Single-member districts by population[e]	Lt. Gov.	Yes		Annual

Proposed Amendments	Salary	Term (in years)	Non-partisan	Size	Elective Districts	Presiding Officer	Initiative	Referendum	Maximum Length of Session	Frequency of Session
OHIO H.J.R. No. 59 (Doyle, Harter, Huml, Hudlett)	To be determined	2		About 100	Multiple-member districts by population	Lt. Gov.	Yes	Yes		Annual
OKLAHOMA H.J.R. No. 10 (Whitaker)	$90,000 a session divided equally	2	Yes	30–50	Single-member districts by population.	Lt. Gov.	Yes	Yes		Biennial
OREGON S.J.R. No. 1 (Carney)	$60,000 a biennium divided equally	2	Yes	30–36	Single-member districts by population. Minimum population 14,000 per district	Elected by legislature	Yes	Yes	Regular session 10 days, special session 3 days, after reading last bill third time	Biennial
OREGON S.J.R. No. 3 (Staples and Burke)	$6 a day up to $360			30	As at present for senators		Yes	Yes	Special session 20 days	
OREGON H.J.R. No. 6 (Oleen and 6 others)	$350 a year	2		60	Single-member districts by population	Elected by legislature	Yes	Yes	Indefinite	
PENNSYLVANIA H.J.R. No. 791 (Marino)	$3000 a year	2	Yes	90–110	Double-member districts by population[d]	Lt. Gov.	Yes	Yes		Annual
PENNSYLVANIA H.J.R. No. 1187 (Harkins)	To be determined	4[b]		200	One-to-four-member districts by population[e]	Elected by legislature				Annual
TEXAS H.J.R. No. 15 (Fox and 10 others)	Maximum $10 a day first 120 days, then $5 a day			100–50	By counties and by population[f]	Lt. Gov.				Biennial
WASHINGTON H.J.R. No. 10 (Ginnett)	$10 a day	2		94–104 (99 1st session)	As for the house at present; districted by population.	Lt. Gov.	Yes	Yes		Annual

									Indefinite	Annual
WASHINGTON S.B. No. 207 S.J.R. No. 11 (Farquharson)	$1500 a year	4[b]		46–60 (46 1st session)	Single-member districts by population	Lt. Gov.	Yes	Yes	Indefinite	Annual
WASHINGTON H.J.R. No. 21 (Heutter)	$400 a month	4[b]		24	6 districts by population; 4 members per district	Gov.	Yes	Yes		Biennial
WASHINGTON H.J.R. No. 28 (Constitutional Revision Committee)	$10 a day	2		95–110 (91 1st session)	As at present for the house; by population except that each county sends at least 1 member	Lt. Gov.	Yes	Yes		
WASHINGTON H.J.R. No. 32 (Gates)	$4000 a year	4[b]		46–60	Single-member districts by population	Lt. Gov.	Yes	Yes		Every other month
WASHINGTON H.B. No. 375 (Vane)	Maximum $27,600 a year divided equally	4[b]		36–46	Single-member districts	Lt. Gov.	Yes	Yes		Biennial
WISCONSIN J.R. No. 11A (Hall)	To be determined	2		90–100	Single-member districts by population		Yes	Yes		
WYOMING S.J.R. No. 1 (Manning)	$30,000 a year divided equally	2	Yes	15–30	Single-member districts by population		Yes			
WYOMING S.J.R. No. 4 (Manning)	$3000 a year	2	Yes	15–30	Single-member districts by population		Yes			

[a] In addition to these, New Mexico S.J.R. No. 4 by Coe provided for a joint committee to study unicameralism and make recommendations at the next session; New York S.R. by Desmond provided for a joint committee to draw up a unicameral bill by February 15, 1938; and Rhode Island, H.B. No. 537 by DiSandro authorized the appointment of a committee to study the feasibility of unicameralism in Rhode Island.

[b] One-half to be elected every two years.

[c] For electing representatives, the districting is more complex. Counties with populations over 200,000 form one group, the rest another. Each group elects one-half the representatives, and the districts are drawn within the group.

[d] Two senators are elected for each one-fiftieth of the state's population and two more for each additional 3/5 of one-fiftieth, unless the adjoining county has between 1/2 and 4/5 of one-fiftieth.

[e] One member for each 1/200th of the state's population in the county or major half of the county. Cities having 1/200th may form a separate district. Each city having one-fiftieth and each county with more than 100,000 population may form a district, electing up to four representatives.

[f] Counties with less than 1/100th–1/150th of the state's population may be added to other districts. Counties over this limit are to elect one representative for each 1/100th–1/150th, up to a total of seven representatives. For a population above 700,000, one representative for each 100,000 is to be elected.

stituents, and the right of recall would safeguard the people against unfaithful or incompetent representatives. Since plans using the longer terms usually adopt the practice of rotating the terms, that is, of electing one-half or one-third of the membership every two years, the continuous presence of experienced legislators is made possible, and newcomers can learn the procedure from those who have been through it before. Blunders should be less frequent under such an arrangement.

Remuneration. — The amendments indicate a general tendency to allow more adequate remuneration for legislators in order that persons may devote a reasonable amount of their time to lawmaking without too much financial sacrifice. The higher salary may also encourage a better class of men to give their services to the state. Eight of the proposals specify that members are to be paid by the day, but it is the more common practice to stipulate an annual salary sum. The suggested rates per day range from $5 to $15. Two proposals provide a monthly salary, one $250 and the other $400. Annual salaries range from $350 to $6,000, with the average falling between $2,000 and $3,000. Where salaries are paid by the year, which is probably as desirable as any arrangement, members receive no additional remuneration for longer or more frequent sessions. Such an arrangement naturally tends to discourage holding or prolonging extra sessions for the sake of monetary returns.

Five proposals adopt the Nebraska practice in specifying lump sums, from $27,000 to $120,000, to be divided equally among the legislators. Virtually all the bills allow the members transportation "to and return" for both regular and special sessions, usually at a maximum rate of ten cents a mile. When members of the legislature serve on a legislative council or in other positions which make extra demands upon their time, especially between sessions, added remuneration should be allowed if they are to accomplish anything constructive.

Frequency of session. — Sixteen of the twenty-six amendments that state how often the legislature is to meet adopt the present general custom of biennial sessions. But the eight bills providing for annual meetings show the unicameralist tendency toward more frequent sessions. These are easily possible in a single chamber and are better adapted to the demands made upon the modern legislature. Financial needs in the states today require an annual consideration of the budget, which, added to other pressing problems, makes annual sessions highly desirable. Two bills are marked by unusual provisions on this subject, one that the legislature must not recess for a period exceeding three months at any time, and the other that the legislature shall convene during alternate months of every year.

Length of session. — Many of the bills fix time limits for the legislative sessions: in two cases 60 days, in one 90 days, in one a double session of 90 and 60 days, and in another 30 and 60 days. One amendment limits the period of assembly by setting a maximum expenditure of $50,000 for the regular session, and three proposals stipulate that special sessions must not exceed twenty days. A more desirable method is that used in the majority of the proposals, leaving the length of session to be determined by the legislature.

Nonpartisan ballots. — Twelve of the proposals prescribe nonpartisan ballots and a thirteenth permits them. Whether it is actually possible to abolish party alignments is doubtful, for some authorities feel that in the instances where a nonpartisan ballot has been used under the bicameral system, it has been ineffective. After a study of the Minnesota election system, Robert E. Cushman concluded that it was nonpartisan in name rather than in practice, because voters frequently ascertain the party affiliations of the candidates before going to the polls and political organizations often endorse candidates openly according to their party membership. But the Nebraska amendment instituted nonpartisan elections, and the results of the first one seem to promise that an approach to the removal of partisan issues has been found.

Whether that promise will be realized is uncertain, and whether it is even desirable is open to disagreement. No one would deny the virtues of the nonpartisan ballot, but whether those virtues are enough to compensate for the loss of leadership that would result from the removal of party lines is a question upon which students of government divide. Senator Norris, for example, is firmly of the opinion that party politics should be eliminated from elections to state legislatures, but Arthur E. Buck believes that even if such elimination were possible, it would be undesirable. William F. Willoughby agrees with Mr. Buck. He says in support of his position:

The party represents the general electorate in a way that the individual members do not. It has no such concern in promoting the interests of particular territorial areas as have the individual members representing such areas. Nor is the pressure of special minority groups upon it as effective as it is when brought to bear upon the individual member. Through the enforcement of party solidarity, moreover, the individual member is, in large measure, protected against the hostility of special interests not supported by his vote through the defense that he can make that his action was dictated by determinations of his party, which, as a good party man, he was under obligations to follow.[3]

Many similar opinions might be cited on both sides of the question.

Initiative and referendum. — Most of the 1937 amendments either retain or institute the initiative and referendum. In a few cases, the provision is for the initiative only

[3] *Principles of Legislative Organization and Administration* (Washington, 1934), p. 57.

and in one case for the referendum only. On the value of these institutions, too, there is room for question. In the words of Professor Dodd, "They have proved neither a panacea for all political ills nor a substitute for representative government." They have proved to be expensive procedures and they are subject to certain abuses.[4] But their value would be increased under unicameralism, because they would serve to limit the powers of the assembly and would be one of the most important checks upon what opponents consider the potential despotism of a unicameral body.

Impeachment. — The procedure for impeachment under unicameralism is another problem dealt with in the amendments. Under the bicameral system the common practice has been for the lower house to bring charges and the upper house to try them. In thirteen of the unicameralist proposals the single chamber both brings and tries the cases, and a few others provide for the charges to be brought by the legislature and tried by the supreme court. The latter was Nebraska's method under her bicameral system and it has been retained under the new form. Two of the Ohio amendments which provide for two classes of legislature members propose that in impeachment cases the charges are to be brought by the county members and tried by the district members. Still another plan has the charges brought by the legislative council and the cases tried by the legislature.

Relation between executive and legislative departments. — One of the objectives of the unicameral system is to establish a closer relationship between the executive and the legislature. Therefore, the amendment-framers should seek for a workable plan which makes possible full cooperation between these two branches of the government. The recent amendments show divergent tendencies in this re-

[4] See above, page 82.

gard. Some are directed toward preserving a complete separation of powers between the executive and legislative departments — the old political theory of the early constitution-makers. The Nebraska amendment belongs to this group. The nonpartisan character given to the legislature in that state is evidence of a definite effort to divorce the governor from any party leadership in the assembly. He is not authorized to call special sessions of the legislature or to determine what it shall consider, although he may still make recommendations in his message and retains the veto power, which is not inconsiderable. In spite of the apparent intention of the amendment, it is open to disagreement whether the governor's position and his influence in directing legislation as observed during the first session of Nebraska's one-house legislature were much different than with the two chambers.

An almost opposite principle underlies those amendments for which the model state constitution of the National Municipal League is the general prototype.[5] Under that constitution the governor, elected for four years, is a member of the legislative council and thus plays an active part in the formulation of legislative policies. He appoints the heads of the executive departments, who are thus directly responsible to him. He and they are given seats in the legislature and are permitted to participate in its deliberations, although not to vote. The governor retains the right of veto as well as the usual executive powers. A modification of this arrangement tending in the same direction is the plan under which the governor selects his administrative heads from among the legislators. These men retain their seats in the legislature but at the same time direct administrative affairs. Working under these administrators are secretaries whose positions are permanent civil service appointments.

[5] See above, pages 98–99.

Of the same general type is the proposal that makes the governor the presiding officer of the legislature and assigns to the legislators the right to elect administrative officials and a lieutenant governor to preside in the governor's absence. Here the governor, as governor, has no veto power because measures become laws when passed by the legislature and signed by its presiding officer. This plan certainly pays no attention to the principle of the separation of powers. It makes the executive a definite part of the legislature and its political leader. This is similar in many respects to the practice in the Canadian provinces, which is based on the parliamentary system.

Most of the recent unicameralist proposals incline toward the first of these tendencies, separation of legislature and executive, though many of them are not so clearly one or the other as these examples we have cited. The majority name the lieutenant governor as the presiding officer or permit the legislators to choose their own. It is not likely that the states will soon be ready to discard a principle which has become an American tradition — the separation of powers.

Legislative councils. — In recent years there has developed a movement for the establishment of legislative councils under the bicameral system, but the support for such councils is much stronger among unicameralists. When planned in detail, these councils are small, having from five to nine members, who are usually to be selected by the legislature from its own membership, although some of the proposals designate the council's personnel more specifically. Such a council should be an important feature in any plan of legislative reorganization and should consist of some of the ablest and best-informed members of the legislature. Making the governor a member of such a council is one of the best devices for securing the desired cooperation between executive and legislature. The legislative council should not be a lawmaking body in any sense of the word. It should serve as a fact-finding commission to carry on research, to make special studies of the state's needs, and to recommend desirable measures to the legislature. Its work should be supplemented by the services of an efficient legislative reference librarian and bill-drafting bureau.

Conclusion. — The arguments presented by the proponents of unicameralism leave little justification for the continuance of a large, unwieldy, two-house legislature in our state governments. The strongest single argument that has been offered to support the bicameral system is that one house serves as a check upon the other and thereby prevents careless and hurried legislation. But the studies that have been made furnish no positive assurance that such is the case. "Investigation has corroborated the impression of observers that slowness in reaching a legislative decision usually does not indicate deliberate consideration so much as procrastination. . . . Some of the time-honored claims of superiority for the bicameral plan have been shown by scientific investigation to be unfounded." [6] "The organization of the state legislature as a unicameral body would not reduce the desirable checks upon state legislative action." [7]

Experience with the unicameral legislature, whether in Nebraska or in some other state which may soon adopt it, will undoubtedly disclose both virtues and vices, though probably neither of them to the extent of justifying present fears on one side and expectations on the other. The unicameral system may be expected to reduce the cost of legislation at the same time that it permits better remuneration and so enables the state to command the services of more capable men. This is possible both because of the

[6] Frank G. Bates and Oliver P. Field, *State Government* (New York, 1928), pp. 140–41.

[7] Walter F. Dodd, *State Government* (New York, 1929), p. 145.

economies due to the smaller membership and because of the reduction of expenditures for offices, secretarial assistance, and the like. The unicameral system would eliminate the evils of the conference committee and the deadlocks and unnecessary delays which occur in the shuffle between the two houses of the bicameral form. It would fix responsibility squarely on the shoulders of the individual, would tend to develop responsible leadership, and would facilitate the reduction of the too-numerous legislative committees. The executive veto, the referendum, the recall, and the judicial review would serve as potential safeguards against any possible abuse of power by a single chamber, except, perhaps, in tumultuous and reckless times. But then a second chamber, as little different from the first as state senates now are, would be a no more effective check.

As Professor Dodd observes, one of the advantages of our federal system of government is that "one state may try an experiment, and other states may profit by studying the results." [8] Nebraska can experiment with the unicameral legislature without any great peril, and other states can watch and analyze the results before discarding their bicameral systems for the single chamber. There is every reason to believe that if the Nebraska experiment shows even a fair degree of success, several other states will adopt unicameral legislatures in the very near future. Some interesting facts as to public opinion on this question came to light in the nation-wide poll conducted by the American Legislators' Association in 1934. The question "Do you think that one-house legislatures would or would not be preferable to two-house legislatures?" was sent to all members of the national Congress and to a representative sampling of the membership of various other groups. The following table is a list of these groups with the result of their vote expressed in percentages:

[8] *Ibid.*, p. 147.

Group	For One-House Legislatures	Against One-House Legislatures
United States representatives	24%	76%
United States senators	31	69
State representatives	34	66
State senators	24	76
Nebraska representatives	20	80
Nebraska senators	38	62
American Bankers Association	31	69
Business executives	45	55
Newspaper editors	41	59
American Bar Association	34	66
Governmental Research Association .	82	18
American Political Science Association	85	15
American Federation of Labor	64	36
League of Women Voters	73	27
American Association of University Women	52	48
Total votes cast	41	59

In general, legislators, bankers, business executives, newspaper editors, and lawyers were opposed to the single house; but government research workers, teachers of political science, organized labor, women voters, and university women favored it. Considering the events that have occurred since that poll was taken, we may safely assert that a similar poll taken today would show less opposition to the single house. In a not-too-distant future the people of the United States may, like the Canadians, support a bicameral legislature for the federal government but demand a single-chamber assembly for state lawmaking. Current opinion and activity may result in bringing about such a development.

APPENDIX I. AMENDMENT TO NEBRASKA CONSTITUTION ADOPTED NOVEMBER 6, 1934

BE IT ENACTED BY THE PEOPLE OF THE STATE OF NEBRASKA:

That Section 1 of Article III of the Constitution of Nebraska be amended to read as follows:

SEC. 1. Commencing with the regular session of the Legislature to be held in January, nineteen hundred and thirty-seven, the legislative authority of the State shall be vested in a Legislature consisting of one chamber. The people reserve for themselves, however, the power to propose laws, and amendments to the Constitution, and to enact or reject the same at the polls, independent of the Legislature, and also reserve power at their own option to approve or reject at the polls any act, item, section, or part of any act passed by the Legislature. All authority vested by the constitution or laws of the State in the Senate, House of Representatives, or joint session thereof, in so far as applicable, shall be and hereby is vested in said Legislature of one chamber. All provision in the constitution and laws of the State relating to the Legislature, the Senate, the House of Representatives, joint sessions of the Senate and House of Representatives, Senator, or member of the House of Representatives, shall, in so far as said provisions are applicable, apply to and mean said Legislature of one chamber hereby created and the members thereof. All references to Clerk of House of Representatives or Secretary of Senate shall mean, when applicable, the Clerk of the Legislature of one chamber. All references to Speaker of the House of Representatives or temporary president of the Senate shall mean Speaker of the Legislature. Wherever any provision of the constitution requires submission of any matter to, or action by, the House of Representatives, the Senate, or joint session thereof or the members of either body or both bodies, it shall after January first, nineteen hundred and thirty-seven, be construed to mean the Legislature herein provided for.

THE UNICAMERAL LEGISLATURE

That Section 5 of Article III of the Constitution of Nebraska be amended to read as follows:

SEC. 5. At the regular session of the Legislature held in the year nineteen hundred and thirty-five the Legislature shall by law determine the number of members to be elected and divide the State into Legislative Districts. In the creation of such Districts, any county that contains population sufficient to entitle it to two or more members of the Legislature shall be divided into separate and distinct Legislative Districts, as nearly equal in population as may be and composed of contiguous and compact territory. After the creation of such districts, beginning in nineteen hundred and thirty-six and every two years thereafter, one member of the Legislature shall be elected from each such District. The basis of apportionment shall be the population excluding aliens, as shown by next preceding federal census. In like manner, when necessary to a correction of inequalities in the population of such districts, the State may be redistricted from time to time, but no oftener than once in ten years.

That Section 6 of Article III of the Constitution of Nebraska be amended to read as follows:

SEC. 6. The Legislature shall consist of not more than fifty members and not less than thirty members. The sessions of the Legislature shall be biennial except as otherwise provided by this constitution or as may be otherwise provided by law.

That Section 7 of Article III of the Constitution of Nebraska be amended to read as follows:

SEC. 7. Members of the Legislature shall be elected for a term of two years beginning at noon on the first Tuesday in January in the year next ensuing the general election at which they were elected. Each member shall be nominated and elected in a non-partisan manner and without any indication on the ballot that he is affiliated with or endorsed by any political party or organization. The aggregate salaries of all the members shall be $37,500 per annum, divided equally among the members and payable in such manner and at such times as shall be provided by law. In addition to his salary, each member shall receive an amount equal to his actual expenses in traveling by the most usual route once to and returning from each regular or special session of the Legislature. Members of the Legislature shall receive no pay nor perquisites other than said salary and expenses, and employees of the Legislature shall receive no compensation other than their salary or per diem.

That Section 10 of Article III of the Constitution of Nebraska be amended to read as follows:

SEC. 10. The Legislature shall meet in regular session at 12:00 o'clock (noon) on the first Tuesday in January in the year next ensuing the election of the members thereof. The Lieutenant Governor shall preside, but shall vote only when the Legislature is equally divided. A majority of the members elected to the Legislature shall constitute a quorum; the Legislature shall determine the rules of its proceedings and be the judge of the election, returns, and qualifications of its members, shall choose its own officers, including a Speaker to preside when the Lieutenant Governor shall be absent, incapacitated, or shall act as Governor. No members shall be expelled except by a vote of two-thirds of all members elected to the Legislature, and no member shall be twice expelled for the same offense. The Legislature may punish by imprisonment any person not a member thereof who shall be guilty of disrespect to the Legislature by disorderly or contemptuous behavior in its presence, but no such imprisonment shall extend beyond twenty-four hours at one time, unless the person shall persist in such disorderly or contemptuous behavior.

That Section 11 of Article III of the Constitution of Nebraska be amended to read as follows:

SEC. 11. The Legislature shall keep a journal of its proceedings and publish them (except such parts as may require secrecy) and the yeas and nays of the members on any question, shall at the desire of any one of them be entered on the journal. All votes shall be viva voce. The doors of the Legislature and of the Committee of the Whole shall be open, unless when the business shall be such as ought to be kept secret.

That Section 14 of Article III of the Constitution of Nebraska be amended to read as follows:

SEC. 14. Every bill and resolution shall be read by title when introduced and a printed copy thereof provided for the use of each member, and the bill and all amendments thereto shall be printed and read at large before the vote is taken upon its final passage. No such vote upon the final passage of any bill shall be taken, however, until five legislative days after its introduction nor until it has been on file for final reading and passage for at least one legislative day. No bill shall contain more than one subject, and the same shall be clearly expressed in the title. And no law shall be amended unless the new act contain the section or sections as amended and the section or sections so amended shall be repealed. The Lieutenant Governor, or the Speaker if acting as presiding officer, shall sign, in the presence of the Legislature while the same is in session and capable of transacting business, all bills and resolutions passed by the legislature.

That Sections 12 and 28, of Article III, and Sections 9 and 17, of Article IV, be and the same hereby are repealed, effective as of January 1, 1937.

APPENDIX II. CONSTITUTIONAL AMENDMENT PROPOSED BY THE OHIO SINGLE-HOUSE LEGISLATURE LEAGUE *

BE IT RESOLVED BY THE GENERAL ASSEMBLY OF THE STATE OF OHIO, three-fifths of the members elected to each house concurring therein, That there be submitted to the electors of the state on the first Tuesday after the first Monday in November, 1937, a proposal to repeal sections 1, 2, 9, 11, 14, 15, 17, 19, 23, 24, 25 and 31 of article II; sections 16 and 17 of article III; and sections 1, 2, 3, 4, 5, 6, 7, 8, 9, 10 and 11 of article XI; and to adopt in lieu thereof sections 1, 2, 9, 14, 19, 23, 24, 25 and 31 of article II of the constitution of the state of Ohio to read as follows:

ARTICLE II

SEC. 1. The legislative power of the state not reserved to the people shall be vested in a general assembly. The general assembly shall consist of a single body of representatives; and shall succeed to all the powers of either, or both, the house of representatives and the senate as heretofore constituted, and shall be subject to all the provisions of the constitution limiting the power or controlling the procedure of either, or both, such houses so far as such provisions may be applicable to a single chamber assembly, and so far as they are consistent with the provisions of this section. Whenever in the constitution reference is made to the house of representatives or to the senate, or both, or to either or both of the houses of the general assembly, or to the members elected thereto, to representatives, or to senators, such provisions so referring shall be deemed to refer to the general assembly and to representatives therein. Whenever action by either the senate or the house of representatives, or both, is required by any section of the constitution, action by the general assembly shall constitute full compliance therewith.

* Introduced in the 1937 session of the legislature as House Joint Resolution No. 59.

The people reserve to themselves the power to propose to the general assembly laws and amendments to the constitution, and to adopt or reject the same at the polls on a referendum vote as hereinafter provided. They also reserve the power to adopt or reject any law, any section of any law or any item in any law appropriating money passed by the general assembly except as hereinafter provided; and independent of the general assembly to propose amendments to the constitution and to adopt or reject the same at the polls. The limitations expressed in the constitution, on the power of the general assembly to enact laws, shall be deemed limitations on the power of the people to enact laws.

SEC. 2. Representatives in the general assembly shall be elected biennially by the electors of the respective assembly districts, in such manner as shall be provided by law. Their terms shall commence on the first day of January next after their election, and shall continue two years. All vacancies which may happen in the general assembly may be filled for the unexpired term in such manner as may be provided by law.

SEC. 9. The general assembly shall keep a correct journal of its proceedings, which shall be published. On demand of any member a roll call shall be taken upon any action of the general assembly and the names of the members voting for or against entered upon the journal. Every committee to which a bill or other matter is referred shall return the same to the general assembly with a report thereon. On passage of every bill a vote shall be taken by yeas and nays and entered on the journal; but except in case of an emergency bill no such vote shall be taken until at least ten days after the same shall have been engrossed in final form and reported to the general assembly. No bill shall be engrossed, or passed into a law, without the concurrence in each case of a majority of all the members of the general assembly.

SEC. 14. The general assembly may establish a legislative council consisting of not more than fifteen members chosen from among the representatives. It shall be the duty of the council to prepare legislation for consideration by the general assembly and to make such investigations and to perform such other duties incident thereto as shall be provided by law or resolution. The general assembly may authorize or empower the council to meet at such periods either during or between sessions of the general assembly as shall be specified by law or resolution. The general assembly may provide by law for additional salary for members of the legislative council and for reimbursing them for their actual traveling expenses on public business directly connected with the duties of the council.

SEC. 19. No member of the general assembly shall during the term for which he shall have been elected or for one year thereafter be appointed to any civil office under this state.

SEC. 23. The governor, lieutenant governor and other elective or appointive executive officers of the state may be removed from office by resolution of the general assembly if two-thirds of the members elected thereto concur therein, but no such removal shall be made until the person sought to be removed shall have been given a statement of the reason for the removal, and an opportunity to be heard. Provisions shall be made by law for the succession to the office of governor in the event of death, removal or disability of both the governor and the lieutenant governor.

SEC. 24. The general assembly shall, within the first three months of the year next following the adoption of this section, and within each year thereafter whose number ends in one, divide the state by law into assembly districts. Each assembly district shall be composed of compact and contiguous territory. In dividing the state into assembly districts, care should be taken to make each district contain as nearly as possible one or more entire ratios of population with the least remaining fraction thereof which it is practicable to obtain. A ratio of population for the purpose of this section shall be one-hundredth part of the population of the state. If no law dividing the state into assembly districts shall have taken effect within three months after any time limited in this section for the general assembly to divide the state into assembly districts, it shall be the duty of the secretary of state forthwith to divide the state into assembly districts and to publish his proclamation thereof in the same manner as a law. At each election in November of the even-numbered years there shall be elected in each assembly district as many representatives as by the most recent United States census such district contains entire ratios of population.

SEC. 25. The general assembly shall convene in regular session annually on the first Monday in January. On petition signed by one-fifth of the members it shall be the duty of the secretary of state, by public proclamation and by notice to each representative, to convene the general assembly in special session on a day specified in the petition, not sooner than thirty days after the last adjournment or recess of the general assembly, nor sooner than fifteen days after the filing of the petition with the secretary of state. At any special session so convened any business which may properly come before the general assembly in regular session may be transacted. Pending legislation and other pending business shall expire only with the term of office of the representatives, except such business as shall be referred to the succeeding session of the general assembly. The lieutenant governor shall be the speaker of each general assembly until and unless otherwise provided by such general assembly. When the lieutenant governor serves as speaker he shall receive the same salary and allowance as a representative of the general assembly.

Sec. 31. The salaries of the members of the general assembly shall be fixed by law and shall be paid in equal monthly installments. In addition to his salary each representative shall be paid mileage between his home and the capital by the most direct route at not more than five cents per mile traveled, not more than once going and once returning each week during which the general assembly actually meets and during which such representative is in actual attendance. No representative, nor officer or employee of the general assembly shall be paid any allowance or perquisite of any kind except as expressly provided herein. No change in the compensation of representatives, officers or employees of the general assembly shall take effect during the legislative term.

At such election herein referred to, the foregoing proposal shall be placed on the official ballot in the manner provided by law in such form as the secretary of state may designate.

If the votes cast for the proposal shall exceed those against it, such amendment shall go into effect on the first day of January, one thousand nine hundred and thirty-eight, and new sections 1, 2, 9, 14, 19, 23, 24, 25 and 31 of article II, as herein proposed, shall take effect, and existing sections 1, 2, 9, 11, 14, 15, 17, 19, 23, 24, 25 and 31 of article II; sections 16 and 17 of article III; and sections 1, 2, 3, 4, 5, 6, 7, 8, 9, 10 and 11 of article XI of the constitution of the state of Ohio shall be thereby repealed.

APPENDIX III. AMENDMENTS PROPOSED
IN CALIFORNIA

RECENT unicameralist amendments proposed in California are of particular interest because of their attempt to solve the problem of rural-urban representation. The following excerpts from three of them contain their principal provisions.

SENATE CONSTITUTIONAL AMENDMENT NO. 6, 1935

Resolved by the Senate, the Assembly concurring, That the Legislature of the State of California, at its fifty-first regular session commencing on January 7, 1935, two-thirds of the members elected to each of the two houses of the said Legislature voting in favor thereof, hereby proposed to the people of the State of California, that the Constitution of said State be amended by adding to Article IV thereof a new section, to be numbered 37, and to read as follows:

SEC. 37. (a) Commencing with the regular session of the Legislature to be held in January, nineteen hundred and thirty-nine, the legislative authority of the State shall be vested in a Legislature of forty members, consisting of one chamber, to be known as "The Legislature of the State of California." The people reserve for themselves, however, the powers of the initiative and the referendum, as hereinabove provided. All authority now vested by the Constitution or laws of the State in the Senate, the Assembly, or joint session thereof, in so far as applicable, shall be and hereby is vested in said Legislature of one chamber. All provisions in the Constitution and laws of the State relating to the Legislature, the Senate, and Assembly, joint sessions of the Senate and Assembly, Senator or member of the Assembly, shall in so far as said provisions are applicable, apply to and mean said Legislature of one chamber hereby created, and the members thereof. All references to clerk of Assembly or secretary of Senate shall mean, when applicable, the secretary of the Legislature of one chamber. All references to speaker of the Assembly or president of the Senate shall mean president of the Legislature. Wherever any provision of the Constitution requires submission of any matter to, or action by, the assembly, the Senate or joint session thereof, or the members of either body or both bodies, it shall, after January 1, 1939, be construed to mean the Legislature herein provided for.

(b) At the regular session of the Legislature held in the year nineteen hundred and thirty-seven, the Legislature shall divide the State into districts in proportion to population, except as herein otherwise provided. In creation of such districts, any county that contains population sufficient to entitle it to two or more members of the Legislature shall be divided into separate and distinct legislative districts, as nearly equal in population as may be, composed of contiguous and compact territory.

After the creation of such districts, beginning in nineteen hundred and thirty-eight, one member of the Legislature shall be elected from each such district, and shall serve for four years; provided, however, that at the election to be held in nineteen hundred and thirty-eight, members from each odd numbered district shall be elected for a period of four years. The basis of apportionment shall be the population, excluding aliens, as shown by the next preceding Federal census. In like manner, when necessary to correction of inequalities in the population of such districts, the State may be redistricted from time to time, but no oftener than once in ten years; provided, however, that in no event shall any one county have more than twenty-five per cent of the members of said one-chamber Legislature. . . .

ASSEMBLY CONSTITUTIONAL AMENDMENT NO. 33, 1937

Resolved by the Senate, the Assembly concurring, That the Legislature of the State of California, at its fifty-second regular session, commencing on the fourth day of January, 1937, two-thirds of all the members elected to each house voting in favor hereof, hereby proposed to the people of the State of California that the Constitution of said State be amended as follows:

That Section 1 of Article IV be amended to read as follows:

SEC. 1. The legislative power of this State shall be vested in a House of Representatives which shall be designated "The Legislature of the State of California," but the people reserve to themselves the power to propose laws and amendments to the

Constitution, and to adopt or reject the same, at the polls independent of the Legislature, and also reserve the power, at their own option, to so adopt or reject any act, or section or part of any act, passed by the Legislature. . . .

That Section 2 of Article IV be amended to read as follows:

SEC. 2. The sessions of the Legislature shall be annual, unless the Governor shall, in the interim, convene the Legislature, by proclamation, in extraordinary session. All sessions, other than extraordinary, shall commence at twelve o'clock M., on the first Monday after the first day of January next succeeding the election of its members, and shall continue in session for a period not exceeding thirty days thereafter; whereupon a recess must be taken for not less than thirty days. On the reassembling of the Legislature, no bill shall be introduced without the consent of three-fourths of the members thereof, nor shall more than two bills be introduced by any one member after such reassembling.

That Section 3 of Article IV be amended to read as follows:

SEC. 3. Members of the Legislature shall be chosen annually and their term of office shall be one year; and each election shall be on the first Tuesday after the first Monday in November, unless otherwise ordered by the Legislature.

That Section 4 of Article IV be amended to read as follows:

SEC. 4. No person shall be a member of the House of Representatives who has not been a citizen and inhabitant of the State three years, and of the district for which he shall be chosen one year, next before his election.

That Section 5 of Article IV be amended to read as follows:

SEC. 5. The House of Representatives shall consist of eighty members, to be elected by districts, numbered as hereinafter provided. . . .

SENATE CONSTITUTIONAL AMENDMENT NO. 21, 1937

That Section 1 of Article IV be amended to read as follows:

SEC. 1. The legislative power of the State shall be vested in a unicameral body which shall be designated the "Legislature of the State of California," but the people reserve to themselves the power to propose laws and amendments to the Constitution and to adopt or reject the same at the polls, independent of the Legislature, and also reserve the power, at their own option, to so adopt or reject any act, or section or part of any act, passed by the Legislature.

That Section 2 of said Article IV be amended to read as follows:

SEC. 2. The Legislature shall assemble annually and hold its sessions for such periods during each year as it shall determine, and take such periodical recesses as it may deem necessary or expedient for the discharge of its duties and the work of its committees. Its first session in each year shall commence at twelve o'clock noon on the first Monday after the first day of January. Any period for which the Legislature has recessed may be terminated and it shall reconvene when called into session by the proclamation of the Governor, or upon a call in writing signed by a majority of its members, and such notice thereof as shall be provided by its rules or by statute. No bill, except any measure initiated by petition and submitted to the Legislature as provided for in section 1 of this article, shall be passed without the consent of three-fourths of the members of the Legislature until the expiration of a period of thirty days after the introduction thereof; whereupon the same may be passed by a majority vote of the members.

That Section 3 of the said Article IV be amended to read as follows:

SEC. 3. After the adoption hereof, members of the Legislature shall be elected on the first Tuesday after the first Monday in November, 1940, and on the same day of each second year thereafter, and shall serve for a term of two years beginning on the first day of January next following their election. . . .

SEC. 5. The Legislature shall consist of eighty members, to be elected by districts numbered as hereinafter provided.

That Section 6 of said Article IV be amended to read as follows:

SEC. 6. For the purpose of choosing members of the Legislature, the State shall be divided into eighty legislative districts composed, subject to the provisions of this section, as nearly equal in population as may be. The legislative districts shall be numbered from one to eighty, inclusive, in numerical order, commencing at the northern boundary of the State and ending at the southern boundary thereof; provided that no county shall be divided into more than thirty legislative districts. In the formation of legislative districts, no county, or city and county, shall be divided unless it contains sufficient population within itself to form two or more districts. Each district shall choose a member of the Legislature. . . . A reapportionment commission, which is hereby created, consisting of the Lieutenant Governor, who shall be chairman, and the Attorney General, Surveyor General, Secretary of State and State Superintendent of Public Instruction, shall forthwith apportion such districts in accordance with the provisions of this section and such apportionment of said districts shall be immediately effective the same as if the act of said reapportionment commission were an act of the Legislature, subject however, to the same provisions of referendum as apply to the acts of the Legislature. . . .

SEC. 7. The Legislature shall choose its own committees and officers, with the exception that the Lieutenant Governor of this State shall be the chief presiding officer. The Legislature shall be the judge of the qualifications, elections and returns of its members. . . .

SEC. 23. The members of the Legislature shall receive for their services the sum of two hundred and fifty dollars each for each month of the term for which they are elected, to be paid monthly, and mileage to be fixed by law, all paid out of the state treasury, such mileage not to exceed ten cents per mile.

That Section 23a of said Article IV be amended to read as follows:

SEC. 23a. The legislature may provide for additional help; but in no case shall the total expenses of officers, employees and attaches exceed the sum of five hundred dollars per day during any of its sessions. The Legislature shall provide for the selection of all officers, employees and attaches and so far as advisable shall require such selection to be under the provisions of the law governing civil service. . . .

SEC. 34. The Governor shall, before January 31, 1937, and biennially thereafter, before January 31 of each second year, submit to the Legislature, with an explanatory message, a budget containing a complete plan and itemized statement of all proposed expenditures of the State provided by existing law or recommended by him. . . .

BIBLIOGRAPHY

BOOKS AND PAMPHLETS

ADAMS, JOHN. *A Defense of the Constitutions of Government of the United States of America, against the Attack of M. Turgot, in His Letters to Dr. Price, 22 March, 1778.* Volumes IV–VI in Charles F. Adams, editor, *The Works of John Adams.* 10 vols. Boston, 1850–56.

ALLYN, EMILY. *Lords versus Commons: A Century of Conflict, 1830–1930.* New York, 1931.

ANDERSON, WILLIAM. *American City Government.* New York, 1925.

BATES, FRANK G., and OLIVER P. FIELD. *State Government.* New York, 1928.

BEARD, CHARLES A. *American Government and Politics.* New York, 1935.

————. *An Economic Interpretation of the Constitution of the United States.* New York, 1929.

BOLLES, ALBERT S. *Pennsylvania, Province and State.* 2 vols. New York, 1899.

BRYCE, JAMES. *The American Commonwealth.* 3d edition. 2 vols. New York, 1893–95.

BUCK, ARTHUR E. *Modernizing Our State Legislatures.* Philadelphia, 1936.

BURGESS, JOHN W. *Political Science and Comparative Constitutional Law.* New York, 1910.

CARROLL, DANIEL B. *The Unicameral Legislature of Vermont.* Montpelier, Vermont, 1933.

CHAMBERLAIN, JOSEPH P. *Legislative Processes: National and State.* New York, 1936.

CHIPMAN, DANIEL. *A Memoir of Thomas Chittenden.* Middlebury, Vermont, 1849.

COLVIN, DAVID L. *The Bicameral Principle in the New York Legislature.* New York, 1913.

CRAWFORD, FINLA GOFF. *State Government.* New York, 1931.

DODD, WALTER F. *State Government.* New York, 1928.

ELLIOT, JONATHAN. *Debates in the Several State Conventions on the Adoption of the Federal Constitution.* 5 vols. Philadelphia, 1836–59.

The Federalist. Numbers 48, 62, and 63.

GALLAGHER, HUBERT R. *Single House Legislatures.* Chicago, 1935.

GARNER, JAMES W. *Introduction to Political Science.* New York, 1910.

HAINES, CHARLES G., and BERTHA M. HAINES. *Principles and Problems of Government.* 3d edition. New York, 1934.

HALL, HILAND A. *History of Vermont from Its Discovery to Its Admission into the Union in 1791.* Albany, 1868.

HICHBORN, FRANKLIN. *The Story of the Session of the California Legislature of 1909.* San Francisco, 1909.

HOLCOMBE, ARTHUR N. *Government in a Planned Democracy.* New York, 1935.

BIBLIOGRAPHY

——. *State Government in the United States.* New York, 1931.

HOSKINS, NATHAN. *A History of the State of Vermont.* Vergennes, Vermont, 1831.

JOHNSON, CLAUDIUS O. *Government in the United States.* New York, 1933.

JONES, CHARLES C. *A History of Georgia.* 2 vols. Boston, 1883.

KENNEDY, W. P. M. *The Constitution of Canada.* London, 1922.

KENT, JAMES. *Commentaries on American Law.* 12th edition. 4 vols. Boston, 1896.

LECKY, WILLIAM E. H. *Democracy and Liberty.* 2 vols. New York, 1896.

LEES-SMITH, HASTINGS B. *Second Chambers in Theory and Practice.* London, 1923.

LIEBER, FRANCIS. *On Civil Liberty and Self Government.* 3d edition. Philadelphia, 1874.

LOGAN, EDWARD. *Lobbying.* Supplement to the *Annals of the American Academy of Political and Social Science,* volume 144. Philadelphia, July, 1929.

LUCE, ROBERT. *Legislative Assemblies.* Boston, 1924.

——. *Legislative Principles.* New York, 1930.

——. *Legislative Problems.* Boston, 1935.

——. *Legislative Procedure.* Boston, 1922.

McBAIN, HOWARD L., AND LINDSAY ROGERS. *The New Constitutions of Europe.* New York, 1922.

M'CALL, HUGH. *The History of Georgia.* Atlanta, 1909.

McHENRY, DEAN E. *Single House Legislatures.* Berkeley, California, 1935.

McKINLEY, ALBERT E. *The Suffrage Franchise in the Thirteen English Colonies in America.* Philadelphia, 1905.

McMASTER, JOHN B., and FREDERICK D. STONE. *Pennsylvania and the Federal Constitution, 1787–1788.* Philadelphia, 1888.

MARRIOTT, J. A. R. *Second Chambers.* London, 1910.

MATHEWS, JOHN MABRY. *American State Government.* New York, 1934.

MERRIAM, CHARLES E. *American Political Ideas.* New York, 1920.

MILL, JOHN STUART. *Representative Government.* New York, 1875.

MORAN, FRANCIS. *The Rise and Development of the Bicameral System in America.* Baltimore, 1895.

OGG, FREDERIC A., and P. ORMAN RAY. *Essentials of American Government.* New York, 1936.

——. *Introduction to American Government.* 4th edition. New York, 1931.

PASQUET, D. *An Essay on the Origins of the House of Commons.* Cambridge, England, 1935.

PATTERSON, CALEB P. *American Government.* New York, 1933.

POLLARD, ALBERT F. *The Evolution of Parliament.* London, 1920.

REED, THOMAS H. *Municipal Government in the United States.* New York, 1934.

REINSCH, PAUL S. *Legislatures and Legislative Methods.* New York, 1907.

RILEY, FRANKLIN L. *Colonial Origins of New England Senates.* Baltimore, 1896.

ROBERTS, G. B. *The Functions of an English Second Chamber.* London, 1926.

ROGERS, LINDSAY. *The American Senate.* New York, 1926.

THE UNICAMERAL LEGISLATURE

SCHAFFTER, DOROTHY. *The Bicameral System in Practice.* Iowa City, 1929.

SENNING, JOHN P. *The One-House Legislature.* New York, 1937.

SHEPHERD, WILLIAM R. *History of Proprietary Government in Pennsylvania.* New York, 1896.

STEVENS, WILLIAM B. *A History of Georgia.* 2 vols. Philadelphia, 1859.

STORY, JOSEPH. *Commentaries on the Constitution of the United States.* 5th edition. 2 vols. Boston, 1891.

TANGER, JACOB, and HAROLD F. ALDERFER. *Pennsylvania Government, State and Local.* Harrisburg, Pennsylvania, 1933.

TEMPERLEY, HAROLD W. V. *Senates and Upper Chambers.* London, 1910.

WALKER, HARVEY. *Law Making in the United States.* New York, 1934.

WILLOUGHBY, WILLIAM F. *The Government of Modern States.* New York, 1936.

————. *Principles of Legislative Organization and Administration.* Washington, 1934.

WILSON, WOODROW. *The State.* Boston, 1890.

WINSLOW, CLINTON I. *State Legislative Committees.* Baltimore, 1931.

WINSOR, MULFORD. *Legislative Assemblies.* Phoenix, Arizona, 1931.

YOUNG, JAMES T. *The New American Government and Its Work.* New York, 1933.

ARTICLES

ARNESON, BEN A. "Do Representatives Represent?" *National Municipal Review,* 16:751–54 (December, 1927).

AYLSWORTH, L. E. "Nebraska's Nonpartisan Unicameral Legislature," *National Municipal Review,* 26:77–81 (February, 1937).

BARCLAY, T. S. "Bifurcation out West," *State Government,* 5:3–6 (April, 1932).

————. "The Split Session of the California Legislature," *California Law Review,* 20:42–58 (November, 1931).

BARNETT, JAMES D. "The Bicameral System in State Legislation," *American Political Science Review,* 9:449–66 (August, 1915).

BARTH, HARRY A. "Our City Councils," *National Municipal Review,* 13:294–99 (May, 1924).

BOOTS, RALPH S. "Our Legislative Mills: Nebraska, How the Legislature Behaves Itself in a State in Which the Individual Members Pride Themselves on Independence of a Tight Political Machine," *National Municipal Review,* 13:111–19 (February, 1924).

BRADFORD, E. A. "Slipshod Legislation," *Yale Law Journal,* 4:103–11 (February, 1895).

BRANHALL, F. D. "This Matter of Over-Legislation," *State Government,* 3:1–6 (July, 1930).

BURDETTE, FRANKLIN L. "Conference Committees in the Nebraska Legislature," *American Political Science Review,* 30:1114–16 (December, 1936).

————. "Nebraska, A Business Corporation," *American Mercury,* 34:360–63 (March, 1935).

CLARK, ARCH B. "The Single-Chamber Legislature of Manitoba," *National Municipal Review,* 13:225–33 (April, 1924).

The Commonwealth (official journal of the Commonwealth Club of California, San Francisco), 12:203, 212, 220, 221, 229, 230, 248 (May 5, 1936).

BIBLIOGRAPHY

CUSHMAN, ROBERT E. "Nonpartisan Nominations and Elections," *Annals of the American Academy of Political and Social Science,* 106:83–96 (March, 1923).

DERN, GEORGE H. "Governors and Legislatures," *State Government,* 4:7–16 (August, 1931).

DODD, WALTER F. "Proposed Reforms in State Government," *American Political Science Review,* 4:243–51 (May, 1910).

DORR, HAROLD M. "A Legislative Council for Michigan," *American Political Science Review,* 28:270–75 (April, 1934).

ENGEL, B. S. "Nebraska's New Unicameral System," *The Scholastic,* 25:15 (January 5, 1935).

ENSLOW, H. R. "State Constitutional Development through Amendment in 1932," *American Political Science Review,* 27:227–36 (April, 1933).

"Epidemic Insane Lawmaking," *Independent,* 110:278 (March 27, 1913).

"Evil of Too Many Laws," *Literary Digest,* 47:566 (October 4, 1913).

EWING, CORTEZ A. M. "Lobbying in Nebraska's Legislature," *Public Opinion Quarterly,* 1:102 (July, 1937).

FAULCONER, J. E. "West Virginia Legislature Destroys Hinton's Council-Manager Charter," *National Municipal Review,* 24:225 (April, 1935).

FIEBELMAN, H. U. "Shall We Abolish the Bicameral Legislature?" *Florida Law Journal,* November, 1934, pp. 168–70.

FINTY, TOM, JR. "Our Legislative Mills: Texas," *National Municipal Review,* 12:649–54 (November, 1923).

FLEMING, ROSCOE. "Senator Norris's Legislature," *Nation,* 144:43–44 (January 9, 1937).

Franklin Hichborn's Legislative Bulletin, Sacramento, January 27, 1917, p. 1.

GALLAGHER, HUBERT R. "Legislative Councils," *National Municipal Review,* 24:147–51, 161 (March, 1935).

GAUS, J. M. "The Wisconsin Executive Council," *American Political Science Review,* 26:914–20 (October, 1932).

GODDEN, G. M. "England's Single-Chamber Experiment," *Fortnightly Review,* 93:409–19 (March, 1910).

"A Good Check for the Riot of Legislation," *World's Work,* 11:6812–13 (November, 1905).

GUILD, FREDERIC H. "Achievements of the Kansas Legislative Council," *American Political Science Review,* 29:636–39 (August, 1935).

HALL, JOHN E. "The Bicameral Principle in the New Mexico Legislature," *National Municipal Review,* 16:185–90, 255–60 (March, April, 1927).

HARD, ANNE. "Nebraska's Unicameral Plan," *Independent Woman,* 14:151 (May, 1935).

HINES, W. D. "Our Irresponsible State Governments," *Atlantic Monthly,* 115:637–47 (May, 1915).

HODGES, GEORGE H. "Common Sense for Commonwealths," *Saturday Evening Post,* 187:3 (June 12, 1915).

HULL, M. D. "Legislative Procedure in Illinois," *American Political Science Review,* 7:239–41 (May, 1913).

"The Ideal Second Chamber," *Review of Reviews,* 49:447 (April, 1914).

"Is Bicameralism Wise?" *Woman Citizen,* 8:24 (February 23, 1924).

THE UNICAMERAL LEGISLATURE

JOHNSON, STEPHEN. "Ohio Legislature," *Law Journal of the Student Bar* (Ohio State University, Columbus, Ohio), 1:121–22 (April, 1935).

KELLY, ALICE. "Flash Voting," *State Government*, 3:7–8 (October, 1930).

LANCASTER, LANE W. "Nebraska Considers a One-House Legislature," *National Municipal Review*, 23:373–76 (July, 1934).

————. "Nebraska Prunes Her Legislature," *Current History*, 41:435–36 (January, 1935).

————. "Nebraska's New Legislature," *Minnesota Law Review*, 22:60–77 (December, 1937).

"The League's Proposed One-House Amendment," *Greater Cleveland*, 12:112 (February 18, 1937).

LIEN, A. J. "A Speed Limit for Legislatures," *State Government*, 4:17–20 (June, 1931).

LYONS, RICHARD J. "Bills, Bills, All Kinds of Bills," *State Government*, 5:11 (January, 1932).

McCARTHY, CHARLES. "Remedies for Legislative Conditions," Proceedings of the American Political Science Association, 1907, pp. 80–102.

MEAD, ELWOOD. "What's Wrong with Legislators?" *Independent*, 89:70–71 (January 8, 1917).

MORGAN, J. H. "Second Chambers," *Contemporary Review*, 97:533–44 (May, 1910).

"Nebraska: R.F.D. to F.D.R.," *Time*, 29:16–18 (January 11, 1937).

"Nebraska's Unicameral Adjourns," *State Government*, 10:131–34 (July, 1937). Evaluations of the first unicameral session by Governor R. L. Cochran, Senator George W. Norris, State Senator E. M. Von Seggern, State Senator O. Edwin Schultz, and Mr. Kenneth R. Keller.

NORRIS, GEORGE W. "One House Legislature," *Annals of the American Academy of Political and Social Science*, 181:50–58 (September, 1935).

————. "One House Legislatures for More Efficient Legislation," *Literary Digest*, 118:8 (October 13, 1934).

————. "Only One House," *State Government*, 7:209–10 (October, 1934).

————. "The Model Legislature," *Congressional Record*, 78 (part 3):3276–80 (February 27, 1934).

————. "The One-House Legislature," *National Municipal Review*, 24:87–89 (February, 1935).

OCCEÑA, JESUS. "A Unicameral Legislature for the Philippines," *Philippine Law Journal*, 13:157–76 (November, 1933).

ODEGARD, PETER H. "Political Parties and Group Pressures," *Annals of the American Academy of Political and Social Science*, 179:68–81 (May, 1935).

OLMSTED, H. M. "Education and Occupations of Legislators," *National Municipal Review*, 24:399 (July, 1935).

ORFIELD, LESTER B. "The Unicameral Legislature in Nebraska," *Michigan Law Review*, November, 1935, pp. 26–36.

PIERCE, JULIAN. "The State That Abolished Its Senate," *Current History*, 16:625–27 (July, 1922).

POLLOCK, JAMES K. "The Regulation of Lobbying," *American Political Science Review*, 21:335–41 (May, 1927).

POPPER, DAVID H. "Creating a Philippine Commonwealth," *Foreign Policy Reports*, 12:234–44 (December 15, 1936).

BIBLIOGRAPHY

PUTNEY, BRYANT. "Unicameral Legislatures," *Editorial Research Reports*, 1:103–19 (February 9, 1935).

ROCKOW, LEWIS. "Bentham on the Theory of Second Chambers," *American Political Science Review*, 22:583–90 (August, 1928).

SCHULL, C. W. "Legislative Council in Michigan," *National Municipal Review*, 22:570–71 (November, 1933).

SCHWARTZ, A. A. "Legislative Laboratories Compared," *State Government*, 3:3–7 (August, 1930).

SENNING, JOHN P. "Nebraska Provides for a One-House Legislature," *American Political Science Review*, 29:69–74 (February, 1935).

SMITH, C. LYSLE. "The Committee System in State Legislatures," *American Political Science Review*, 12:607–39 (November, 1918).

"Spotlight on 3000 Committees," *State Government*, 4:3–6 (August, 1931).

STRAIN, C. S. "The Kansas Legislative Council," *American Political Science Review*, 27:800–03 (October, 1933).

———. "The Kansas Legislative Council," *National Municipal Review*, 22:462–63 (September, 1933).

"Tangle of Government," *Saturday Evening Post*, 205:20 (August 20, 1932).

TOLL, HENRY W. "Should We Pay Lawmakers?" *State Government*, 4:11–13 (February, 1931).

———. "The Forty-Eight," *State Government*, 3:2–11 (May, 1930).

———. "What 6620 Legislators Are Thinking About," *National Municipal Review*, 24:7–10, 26 (January, 1935).

"Two Chambers or One?" *Quarterly Review*, 213:234–36 (July, 1910).

"Two Houses or One?" *State Government*, 7:207–08 (October, 1934).

"Unicameral Government," *Independent*, 74:678 (March 27, 1913).

"Unicameral Legislature," *Law Notes*, 35:223 (March, 1932).

WALLACE, S. C. "Government by Committee," *Woman Citizen*, 8:12 (February 9, 1924).

WATTS, I. A. "Why Pennsylvania Abandoned Unicameralism," *State Government*, 9:54–55 (March, 1936).

WEST, VICTOR J. "Our Legislative Mills: California, Home of the Split Session," *National Municipal Review*, 12:369–75 (July, 1923).

"What's Wrong with Our State Legislatures?" *National Municipal Review*, 16:490–91 (August, 1926).

WHITE, HOWARD. "Can Legislatures Learn from City Councils?" *American Political Science Review*, 21:95–100 (February, 1926).

"The Whys of a One-House Legislature," *Greater Cleveland*, 12:109–11 (February 18, 1937).

WILBUR, JAMES B. "The Making of the Republic of Vermont, the Fourteenth State," Proceedings of the American Antiquarian Society, 1921, pp. 359–67.

WRONG, GEORGE M. "The Single-House Legislature of Ontario," *National Municipal Review*, 13:169–72 (March, 1924).

REPORTS, RECORDS, AND DOCUMENTS

A Model State Constitution, National Municipal League, New York, 1921.

Colonial Records of Connecticut, 1689–1706.

Colonial Records of Pennsylvania, volumes XI–XVI.

THE UNICAMERAL LEGISLATURE

Concessions of the Lords Proprietors of New Jersey, 1664–1665.

Documentary Source Book in American Government and Politics, compiled by Cortez A. M. Ewing and Royden J. Dangerfield. New York, 1931.

Documentary Source Book of American History, edited by William Macdonald. New York, 1921.

Documents Illustrative of the Formation of the Union of the American States, selected and arranged by Charles C. Tansill. Washington, D.C., 1927.

Federal and State Constitutions, Colonial Charters and Organic Laws of the United States, compiled by Perley Poore. Washington, D.C., 1878.

FESLER, MAYO. "Another Legislative Debacle in Ohio, the Worst General Assembly at a Time When the State Needed the Best." Unpublished manuscript.

Governor's Message to the Minnesota Legislature, 1935.

Governor's Message to the Nebraska Legislature, January 7, 1937.

GUILD, FREDERIC H. *Expediting Legislative Procedure.* Research report of the Kansas Legislative Council, Topeka, 1935.

Handbook of Information for Members of the California Legislature, compiled by the California State Library, Sacramento, 1937.

Journal of Congress, volume II.

Massachusetts Records, volume I.

Messages to the Kansas Legislature, 1913.

Minnesota Legislative Manual, 1937.

Nebraska Journal of the Constitutional Convention, 1919–1920.

Patent for Providence Plantation, 1643.

Pennsylvania Constitutional Convention: Proceedings Relative to the Calling of the Conventions of 1776 and 1790.

Proceedings of the Assembly of Massachusetts, 1637–1638.

Proceedings of the Nebraska Constitutional Convention, 1917–1920.

Records of the Council of Safety and the Governor and Council of the State of Vermont, 1873.

Report of the New York Bureau of Municipal Research, in the *Nevada State Journal,* November 20, 1924.

Vermont State Papers; Records and Documents, compiled and published by William Slade. Middlebury, Vermont, 1823.

PROPOSED CONSTITUTIONAL AMENDMENTS RELATING TO UNICAMERAL LEGISLATURES

Alabama
Constitutional Amendment, 1935

Arkansas
House Joint Resolution No. 1, 1937

California
Assembly Constitutional Amendment No. 57, 1913
Assembly Constitutional Amendment No. 64, 1913
Assembly Constitutional Amendment No. 66, 1913
Assembly Constitutional Amendment No. 91, 1913
Assembly Constitutional Amendment No. 93, 1913

BIBLIOGRAPHY

Senate Constitutional Amendment No. 73, 1913
Assembly Constitutional Amendment No. 38, 1915
Assembly Constitutional Amendment No. 49, 1915
Senate Constitutional Amendment No. 16, 1915
Assembly Constitutional Amendment No. 25, 1917
Senate Constitutional Amendment No. 8, 1917
Senate Constitutional Amendment No. 18, 1921
Assembly Constitutional Amendment No. 37, 1923
Senate Constitutional Amendment No. 34, 1923
Senate Constitutional Amendment No. 15, 1925
Senate Constitutional Amendment No. 6, 1935
Assembly Constitutional Amendment No. 69, 1935
Assembly Constitutional Amendment No. 28, 1937
Assembly Constitutional Amendment No. 33, 1937
Senate Constitutional Amendment No. 4, 1937
Senate Constitutional Amendment No. 21, 1937

Georgia
House Bill No. 280, 1937

Idaho
House Joint Resolution No. 8, 1937

Iowa
House Joint Resolution No. 3, 1935
Senate Joint Resolution No. 2, 1935
House Joint Resolution No. 4, 1937

Kansas
Senate Concurrent Resolution No. 4, 1935
Senate Concurrent Resolution No. 5, 1937
Senate Concurrent Resolution No. 9, 1937

Maine
House Proposal No. 1327, 1935

Massachusetts
House Constitutional Amendment No. 78, 1936
House Constitutional Amendment No. 1003, 1936
House Constitutional Amendment No. 1081, 1937

Minnesota
House File No. 214, 1937
House File No. 1091, 1937
Senate Bill, No. 197, 1937
Senate Bill No. 452, 1937

Missouri
House Joint and Concurrent Resolution No. 2, 1935
House Joint and Concurrent Resolution No. 4, 1935

Montana
House Bill No. 26, 1935
House Bill No. 73, 1937

Nevada
 Assembly Joint Resolution No. 20, 1937
 Assembly Joint Resolution No. 22, 1937

New Jersey
 Senate Concurrent Resolution No. 1, 1937

New Mexico
 Senate Joint Resolution No. 4, 1937
 Senate Joint Resolution No. 5, 1937

New York
 Senate Resolution, 1936
 Senate Resolution, 1937

North Dakota
 House Concurrent Resolution "R," 1937

Ohio
 House Joint Resolution No. 10, 1937
 House Joint Resolution No. 11, 1937
 House Joint Resolution No. 16, 1937
 House Joint Resolution No. 26, 1937
 House Joint Resolution No. 59, 1937

Oklahoma
 House Joint Resolution No. 10, 1937

Oregon
 House Joint Resolution No. 14, 1935
 Senate Joint Resolution No. 1, 1935
 Senate Joint Resolution No. 14, 1935
 House Joint Resolution No. 6, 1937
 Senate Joint Resolution No. 1, 1937
 Senate Joint Resolution No. 3, 1937

Pennsylvania
 House Joint Resolution No. 791, 1937
 House Joint Resolution No. 1187, 1937

Rhode Island
 House Resolution No. 537, 1937

Texas
 House Joint Resolution No. 43, 1935
 House Joint Resolution No. 15, 1937

Washington
 House Joint Resolution No. 5, 1933
 House Bill No. 675, 1935
 House Bill No. 375, 1937
 House Joint Resolution No. 10, 1937
 House Joint Resolution No. 21, 1937
 House Joint Resolution No. 28, 1937
 House Joint Resolution No. 32, 1937
 Senate Bill No. 207, 1937
 Senate Joint Resolution No. 11, 1937

BIBLIOGRAPHY

Wisconsin

Joint Resolution No. 131S, 1929
Joint Resolution No. 48A, 1931
Joint Resolution No. 26A, 1933
Joint Resolution No. 10A, 1935
Joint Resolution No. 11A, 1935
Substitute Amendment No. 1A to Joint Resolution No. 11A, 1935
Amendment No. 1A to Substitute Amendment No. 1A to Joint Resolution No. 11A, 1935
Amendment No. 2A to Substitute Amendment No. 1A to Joint Resolution No. 11A, 1935
Joint Resolution No. 95A, 1935
Substitute Amendment No. 1A to Joint Resolution No. 95A, 1935
Amendment No. 1A to Substitute Amendment No. 1A to Joint Resolution No. 95A, 1935
Joint Resolution No. 11A, 1937

Wyoming

Senate Joint Resolution No. 1, 1937
Senate Joint Resolution No. 4, 1937

INDEX

Accountability, *see* Responsibility
Adams, John, defense of bicameralism, 30n; on single chamber, 48, 49–50
Advantages of bicameral system, *see* Bicameral system, arguments for
Alabama, 97
Alameda County (California), representation, 65–66, 121
Alberta, 17
Amending of laws, extent of, 60
Amendments, constitutional, in California, 120; unicameralist, *see* Unicameralist proposals
American Legislators' Association, aid to legislators, 84; poll on unicameral system, 163–64
Arizona, 66, 67; the unicameralist movement, 97, 103–08; recall of judges, 103; bicameral legislature, 104–105; advantages of proposed unicameral reorganization, 107–08
Aylsworth, L. E., on caliber of legislators in Nebraska's single chamber, 137

Ballot, nonpartisan, *see* Nonpartisan ballot
Ballot, short, in Nebraska, 141
Beard, Charles A., on caliber of legislators, 77
Bentham, Jeremy, attack on bicameral system, 4n
Bicameral system, origin of term, 4n; origin in English Parliament, 4–5; spread from England, 11, 14, 21, 26; re-established in France, 13–14; origin and development in American colonies, 19–22, 23; traditional in United States, 19, 31, 43–44,

53–54; adoption in federal Congress, 25–30, 31; in federal Congress, not under attack, 25, 64; adopted in Georgia, 33; adopted in Pennsylvania, 37; adopted in Vermont, 39–41; compared with unicameral in Vermont, 41–42; development of theoretical defense for, 45–46; Kent on, 46, 47–48; Bryce on, 46, 51–52; Story on, 47n; studied in practice by Dorothy Schaffter, 59; reform improbable, 75, 76–77, 102, 103, 108; proposed reforms within, 77–88; in city councils, 93–94; compared with single chamber in Nebraska, 142
arguments against, 5, 54–74; of French philosophers, 6; of opponents of House of Lords, 10–11; in Arizona, 104–05; in Ohio, 113; in Nebraska, 135–36. *See also* Unicameral system, arguments for
arguments for, 45–54; advanced by Federalists, 26–30; offered in Vermont, 40; not justified by Vermont experience, 41–43; depend on difference between houses, 64; questioned, 162. *See also* Unicameral system, arguments against
Bill-drafting service, 83, 84, 88, 141, 162
Bills, surplus, 58–59; disposal, 69, 111–12; in conference committee, 72–73, 129–30; number limited, 80; private, 81, 147–48; time limited for introduction, 84–85, 134, 141 (*see also* Split session); time limited for passage, 105, 119, 121

INDEX

135; in unicameralist proposals, 107, 115, 152–55, 158–59; in California, 121n; check on single chamber, 159

Institute of Public Administration, aid to legislators, 84

Inyo County (California), 122

Irish Free State, 15

Italy, 15

Jacobins, 45. *See also* France, unicameral legislatures

Jefferson, Thomas, on purpose of two houses, 23–24

Judicial review, check on legislature, 27, 93, 163; in Missouri, 81; preceding passage of bills, 126

Jugoslavia, 15

Kansas, 131; end-of-session rush, 57; legislative council, 82, 83; unicameralist movement, 96–97

Kent, Chancellor James, on unicameralism, 45–46, 50; on bicameralism, 48

Kentucky, committees, 68

Labor, supports unicameralism, 9, 103, 119, 164

Labor party, English, 9

Lagthing, 16

Lancaster, Lane W., on Nebraska's bicameral legislature, 130

Lancaster County (Nebraska), representation, 136

Latvia, 15

Law and legislative reference bureau, *see* Legislative reference bureau

Laws, stability, 41–42; repealed or amended, 60; vetoed, 61. *See also* Bills; Legislation

Lecky, William E., contributes to bicameralist theory, 45; on despotism of one house, 50

Legislation

costs of, 67–68; in Ohio session of *1935*, 68, 110–11; in six states compared, 110. *See also* Contingent expenses; Mileage; Salaries

reforms proposed to improve, 77–78

review of

by second chamber, in practice, 42, 59–63, 93; in theory, 46–49, 51–52

under unicameral system, 92–93, 140. *See also* Judicial review; Recall; Referendum; Veto, executive

See also Bills, Laws, Legislature, Procedure

Legislative council, 16, 88; in bicameral legislatures, 82; personnel, 82–83, 99, 106, 115, 161; functions, 82, 83, 99, 106, 115, 161–62; in Kansas, 82, 83; in unicameralist proposals, 82, 99, 105, 106–07, 115, 118, 161–62; in Nebraska's single chamber, 141; size, 161

Legislative procedure, *see* Procedure

Legislative reference bureau, aid to legislative council, 83; functions, 83–84; in unicameralist proposals, 88, 115

Legislators, early qualifications, 23–25; caliber, 68, 77–78, 107, 136–37 (*see also* Salaries); public confidence in, 68, 74–75, 94; in poll on unicameral system, 164

Legislature, fear of, 27, 119–20; functions, 49, 52, 90–92; checks on, 49–51 (*see also* Legislation, review of); duties delegated to committees, 70–71; ideal, 76; bicameral, *see* Bicameral system; relation to executive, *see under* Executive; unicameral, *see* Unicameral system

Liberal party, English, 8

Lister, Governor Ernest, of Washington, recommends unicameralism, 97

Lithuania, 15

Lloyd George budget of *1909*, 9

Lobbies, checked by second chamber, 51–52; Story on, 52; aided by committees, 70–71; aided by conference committee, 72; in split session, 86, 120; regulation of, 86–87;

INDEX

New York, 58, 85, 151; colonial legislature, 20n; early suffrage, 24; claims Vermont territory, 37n; end-of-session rush, 55; study of legislature by David L. Colvin, 55, 59; second-chamber check, 59; party rivalry, 62–63; special legislation, 81; governor in legislation, 85; proposed reports on bills, 88; unicameralist amendments, 97, 108n, 155n

New York City, council, 93

Ninety-first General Assembly of Ohio, *see under* Ohio

Nonpartisan ballot, proposed reform, 80; in Minnesota, 80, 157–58; in Nebraska, 80, 134; not a guaranty of nonpartisanship, 80, 157–58; in unicameral system, 88; Senator Norris on, 133; in unicameralist proposals, 152–55, 157–58. *See also* Parties, political

Nonpartisanship, not ensured by nonpartisan ballot, 80, 157–58; in Nebraska's single chamber, 136–37, 139, 143–44, 158, 160; desirability questioned, 158. *See also* Parties, political

Norbeck, Governor, of South Dakota, on unicameralism, 98

Norris, Senator George W., of Nebraska, 19; on size of legislature, 67, 132; on conference committee, 72–73, 132; on economy of unicameral system, 90, 132; unicameralist leader, 132–33; on term of office, 133, 151; on nonpartisan ballot, 133, 158; addresses opening Nebraska unicameral session, 138; approves Nebraska unicameral session, 145

North Carolina, beginnings of bicameral system, 20; early suffrage, 23

Norway, legislature, 16

Nova Scotia, 17

Odelsthing, 16

Ohio, rural-urban problem, 66, 116–17, 151; legislative procedure, 69; unicameralist movement, 95, 114–19; proposed impeachment procedure, 159

Ninety-first General Assembly, *1935:* end-of-session rush, 53, 110; party rivalry, 63, 112; costs, 68, 110–11; committees, 68, 69, 113; delay in legislation, 109–10; disposal of bills, 111–12; summary of defects, 113; impetus to reform, 113–14

Ohio Chamber of Commerce, 114

Ohio Single-House Legislature League, unicameralist amendment, 117–19; text, 169–72

Oklahoma, unicameralist movement, 97

Olson, Governor Floyd B., of Minnesota, on single chamber, 100

Ontario, 15, 17

Oregon, unicameralist movement, 95, 96

Panama, 16

Parliament, English, importance in development of legislative organization, 3–4; origin of bicameral system, 4–5; influence in spread of bicameral system, 5–6, 14, 21, 26; increasing power of lower house, 6–10; unicameral body, 6–7, 10. *See also* House of Commons; House of Lords

Parliament Act of *1911*, 6, 9–10

Parties, political: rivalry delays legislation, 8, 62–63, 112; concurrence destroys second-chamber check, 8, 62; in early Vermont, 39, 40, 42; aided by committees, 70–71; aided by conference committee, 72; control of legislature, 74; selection of candidates, 79; not needed in state government, 133; in Nebraska's single chamber, 136–37, 143–44; defense of, 158. *See also* Nonpartisanship

Pennsylvania, 19, 21, 22, 31, 37; early suffrage, 24, 35; in federal convention, 30; Centinel letters, 30–31; colonial legislature, 33–34; uni-